The Power of NLP:

Rewire Your Reality

Adam Musselli

The Power of NLP:

NEURO-LINGUISTIC PROGRAMMING

Rewire Your Reality

"UNLOCK YOUR POTENTIAL, STAY
FOCUSED. ACHIEVE YOUR GOALS!"

Ψ

ADAM MUSSELLI

ISBN: 978-0-6459235-2-0

©

COPYRIGHTS

CONTENTS

THE POWER OF NLP: REWIRE YOUR REALITY

Foreword

Welcome to a journey that has the potential to transform your life in ways you may have never imagined. This book is your gateway to the extraordinary world of Neuro-Linguistic Programming (NLP), a dynamic and life-changing discipline that can propel you towards personal and career success.

My own journey with NLP began during my days as a psychology student in the mid-2000s. It was a time of discovery, of uncovering the profound influence our thoughts, words, and actions have on our lives. As I delved deeper into NLP and the world of hypnosis, I realized the immense power these disciplines held. They became not only my academic pursuits but also the compass guiding my career as a psychologist, and later to training and education.

Through NLP, I witnessed the incredible transformation it could bring to individuals grappling with self-doubt, anxiety, and limiting beliefs. It enabled me to help patients rewrite their life stories, break free from the chains of their past, and embrace newfound confidence and empowerment.

In this book, you will discover the boundless potential of NLP. It will empower you to communicate effectively, build lasting connections, prioritize your health, and achieve financial prosperity. It's a journey that promises to unlock the doors to your personal and career success.

So, I urge you to embark on this adventure with an open heart and a desire to learn. NLP is not just a set of techniques; it's a way of life that can empower you to rewrite your story and reshape your reality. Your journey starts here, and it has the potential to lead you to a life of unparalleled success.

With enthusiasm for your transformation,

***

INTRODUCTION

In a world filled with endless possibilities and opportunities, the key to unlocking your full potential lies within the intricate workings of your mind. Welcome to "The Power of NLP: Rewire Your Reality," a transformative journey into the realm of Neuro-Linguistic Programming (NLP).

NLP, or Neuro-Linguistic Programming, is a groundbreaking approach to understanding and harnessing the power of human consciousness. It's a dynamic blend of psychology, linguistics, and neurology, and it has the potential to reshape your reality in ways you never thought possible.

Imagine having the ability to reprogram your thoughts, beliefs, and behaviors to align with your goals and desires. Picture yourself communicating with others more effectively, building deeper connections, and mastering the art of persuasion. Envision a life where fear and self-doubt no longer hold you back, where you are in complete control of your destiny. This is the promise of NLP.

"The Power of NLP: Rewire Your Reality" is your guide to tapping into the incredible potential of NLP. Whether you're seeking personal growth, improved relationships, or professional success, this book will equip you with the tools and techniques to create lasting, positive change in your life.

In this journey, we'll explore the core principles of NLP, demystifying its secrets and making them accessible to you. We'll delve into the power of language and how it shapes our thoughts and actions. You'll learn how to identify and reframe limiting beliefs, unlocking the door to your unlimited potential. We'll also delve into the fascinating world of sensory perception, helping you to see the world through a new lens.

But "The Power of NLP" is more than just theory. It's a practical guide, filled with exercises, real-life examples, and actionable strategies that you can apply immediately. Each chapter is designed to take you one step closer to mastering the art of NLP and rewiring your reality.

Are you ready to embark on this extraordinary journey of self-discovery and transformation? Prepare to challenge your assumptions, break through your limitations, and unlock the infinite power of your mind. "The Power of NLP: Rewire Your Reality" is your ticket to a life of purpose, passion, and limitless possibilities.

Your journey starts now.

CHAPTER ONE

INTRODUCTION TO NEURO-LINGUISTIC PROGRAMMING N.L.P

Neuro-Linguistic Programming (NLP) is a versatile and powerful approach to understanding human behavior, communication, and personal development. It explores the intricate connection between neurological processes, language patterns, and behavioral patterns. NLP techniques are widely used in therapy, coaching, and self-improvement to enhance communication, overcome limitations, and achieve personal goals.

What is Neuro-Linguistic Programming?

Neuro-Linguistic Programming, commonly known as NLP, is a powerful and transformative approach to personal and professional development. It is a methodology that explores the relationship between our thoughts, language, and behavior, and how we can use this understanding to unlock our full potential and achieve success in all areas of life.

At its core, NLP is based on the belief that our experiences are shaped by our perception of the world and the way we communicate with ourselves and others. By understanding and harnessing the power of our mind and language, we can reprogram our thoughts, beliefs, and behaviors to create positive change and achieve our goals.

NLP draws upon various disciplines, including psychology, linguistics, and cognitive science, to provide a comprehensive framework for personal growth and transformation. It offers a set of practical tools and techniques that can be applied in various contexts, such as business, relationships, health, and personal development.

One of the fundamental principles of NLP is that our subjective experience of reality is shaped by our internal representations, or the way we perceive and interpret the world around us. These internal representations are constructed through our senses, such as visual images, auditory sounds, kinesthetic sensations, and even our internal dialogue.

NLP teaches us how to become more aware of our internal representations and how to modify them to create more empowering and resourceful states of mind. By changing the way we represent our experiences, we can change our emotional responses, beliefs, and behaviors, ultimately leading to greater success and fulfillment.

Another key aspect of NLP is the study of language patterns and how they influence our thinking and communication. NLP practitioners have identified specific language patterns that can be used to create rapport, influence others, and facilitate positive change. By mastering these language patterns, we can become more effective communicators and influencers in both personal and professional settings.

NLP also emphasizes the importance of modeling excellence. By studying and replicating the strategies and behaviors of successful individuals, we can learn how to achieve similar results in our own lives. This process of modeling allows us to identify the underlying patterns of success and apply them to our own goals and aspirations.

In summary, NLP is a powerful approach to personal and professional development that explores the relationship between our thoughts, language, and behavior. It provides practical tools and techniques for reprogramming our minds, improving our communication skills, and achieving success in all areas of life. Whether you want to enhance your career, improve your relationships, or achieve optimal health and well-being, NLP offers a comprehensive framework for unlocking your full potential and creating the life you desire. In the following sections of this book, we will delve deeper into the history and evolution of NLP, explore its applications in various areas of life, and provide practical exercises and strategies for harnessing its power. Get ready to embark on a transformative journey of self-discovery and personal growth as we unlock the potential of Neuro-Linguistic Programming.

The History and Evolution of NLP

Neuro-Linguistic Programming (NLP) is a powerful approach to personal and professional development that has its roots in the 1970s. It was developed by Richard Bandler, a computer scientist, and John Grinder, a linguist. Together, they sought to understand and model the patterns of excellence in human behavior and communication.

The origins of NLP can be traced back to the work of several influential figures in the fields of psychology and therapy. One of the key influences was the work of Milton Erickson, a renowned psychiatrist and hypnotherapist. Erickson was known for his ability to create rapid and lasting change in his clients through the use of language and communication techniques. Bandler and Grinder studied Erickson's methods and incorporated them into the framework of NLP.

Another significant influence on the development of NLP was the work of Virginia Satir, a family therapist. Satir believed that effective communication and healthy relationships were essential for personal growth and development. Bandler and Grinder studied Satir's techniques and incorporated them into the NLP model.

Bandler and Grinder also drew inspiration from the field of linguistics, particularly the work of Noam Chomsky. Chomsky's theories on transformational grammar and the structure of language provided a foundation for understanding how language influences our thoughts, emotions, and behaviors. Bandler and Grinder applied these linguistic principles to develop techniques for creating change at the subconscious level.

The early years of NLP were marked by a series of workshops and training programs led by Bandler and Grinder. These workshops attracted individuals from various fields, including psychology, therapy, education, and business. Participants were eager to learn the practical applications of NLP and how it could be used to enhance their personal and professional lives.

As NLP gained popularity, Bandler and Grinder began to publish books and training materials to make the principles and techniques of NLP more accessible to a wider audience. Their first book, "The Structure of Magic," introduced the concepts of NLP and provided practical exercises for readers to apply in their own lives.

Over time, NLP evolved and expanded beyond its original foundations. Practitioners began to develop their own techniques and approaches based on the principles of NLP. This led to the emergence of different branches and applications of NLP, such as Neuro-Semantics, Neuro-Hypnotic Repatterning, and New Code NLP.

Today, NLP is widely recognized as a powerful tool for personal, career and professional development. It is used in various fields, including therapy, coaching, education, business, and sports performance. NLP techniques are employed to enhance communication skills, improve relationships, overcome limiting beliefs, manage emotions, and achieve goals.

The evolution of NLP has also been influenced by advancements in neuroscience and cognitive psychology. Research in these fields has provided a deeper understanding of how the brain processes information and how thoughts and behaviors are formed. This knowledge has been integrated into the NLP framework, allowing for more effective and efficient techniques for creating change.

In recent years, NLP has gained recognition as a valuable tool for leadership development and organizational change. Many companies and business leaders have embraced NLP principles and techniques to enhance their communication skills, build effective teams, and drive success.

The history and evolution of NLP demonstrate its enduring relevance and effectiveness in helping individuals unlock their potential and achieve success in all areas of life. By understanding the origins and principles of NLP, you can harness its power to transform your own life and career. In the following sections, we will explore the practical applications of NLP and how it can be used to create positive change in your personal and professional life.

Understanding the Power of NLP in Personal and Professional Life

Neuro-Linguistic Programming (NLP) is a powerful tool that can have a profound impact on both your personal and professional life. By understanding and harnessing the power of NLP, you can unlock your potential and achieve success in various areas, including health, wealth, career, relationships, communication, and personal development.

At its core, NLP is a methodology that explores the relationship between our thoughts, language, and behavior. It provides practical techniques and strategies to help individuals reprogram their minds and create positive change. By understanding how our minds work and learning to communicate effectively with ourselves and others, we can overcome limitations, achieve our goals, and live a more fulfilling life.

One of the key principles of NLP is that our subjective experience of the world is shaped by our internal representations. These representations are made up of our thoughts, beliefs, values, and memories. By becoming aware of these internal representations and learning to change them, we can transform our perception of reality and create new possibilities for ourselves.

In the personal realm, NLP can help you overcome limiting beliefs and develop a positive mindset. It provides techniques for setting compelling goals, reframing negative experiences, managing emotions, and creating empowering habits. By using visualization and mental rehearsal, you can program your mind for success and achieve your desired outcomes. NLP also offers strategies for building confidence and self-esteem, allowing you to step into your full potential and live a life of purpose and fulfillment.

In the professional realm, NLP can be a game-changer. It provides tools for effective communication, leadership, and influence. By mastering the art of rapport and active listening, you can build strong relationships and connect with others on a deeper level. NLP also offers persuasive language patterns that can help you influence and persuade others in a positive way. These skills are invaluable in business settings, where effective communication and leadership are essential for success.

NLP can also enhance your decision-making abilities and negotiation skills. By understanding the strategies and patterns of successful decision-makers, you can make more informed choices and achieve better outcomes. NLP techniques can also be applied to negotiation and conflict resolution, allowing you to find win-win solutions and build mutually beneficial relationships.

Furthermore, NLP can be applied to improve your presentation skills. By understanding the power of non-verbal communication and using persuasive language patterns, you can deliver impactful presentations that captivate your audience and convey your message effectively. NLP techniques can help you overcome stage fright, boost your confidence, and become a more engaging and influential speaker.

In the realm of health and wellness, NLP can have a profound impact. It recognizes the mind-body connection and provides techniques for overcoming bad habits, managing stress, and creating a positive mindset. By using NLP techniques, you can break free from unhealthy patterns, develop new habits that support your well-being, and manage stress effectively. NLP can also help you cultivate a positive mindset, which is essential for maintaining good mental and physical health.

In the realm of relationships, NLP offers valuable insights and techniques. It helps you understand relationship dynamics and provides strategies for effective communication. By learning to communicate with empathy and understanding, you can build strong and harmonious relationships. NLP also provides tools for resolving conflicts and building trust and intimacy, allowing you to create deep and meaningful connections with others.

Taking NLP to the next level involves exploring advanced techniques and applications. Regression, for example, is a powerful NLP technique that allows you to release negative emotions and limiting beliefs from the past. By revisiting past experiences and reframing them, you can free yourself from emotional baggage and create a more empowering future. NLP also offers modeling excellence, which involves studying and replicating the strategies and behaviors of successful individuals. By modeling excellence, you can accelerate your own growth and achieve success in various areas of your life.

NLP is not only a powerful tool for personal and professional development but also a valuable resource for coaches and therapists. It provides techniques and strategies that can be used to facilitate positive change in others. By incorporating NLP into coaching and therapy practices, professionals can help their clients overcome limitations, achieve their goals, and live a more fulfilling life.

In conclusion, NLP is a powerful methodology that can unlock your potential and transform your life. By understanding the power of NLP and applying its techniques and strategies, you can achieve success in various areas, including health, wealth, career, relationships, communication, and personal development. Whether you are looking to overcome limiting beliefs, improve your communication skills, or achieve your goals, NLP can provide you with the tools and insights you need to create positive change and live a life of fulfillment and success.

How NLP Can Transform Your Life and Career

Neuro-Linguistic Programming (NLP) is a powerful tool that can have a profound impact on your life and career. By understanding and harnessing the power of NLP, you can unlock your full potential and achieve success in all areas of your life. Whether you want to improve your communication skills, build better relationships, advance in your career, or enhance your personal development, NLP provides a framework for transformation and growth.

The Power of NLP

NLP is based on the belief that our thoughts, language, and behaviors are interconnected and influence each other. By understanding and working with these connections, we can reprogram our minds and create positive change. NLP techniques and strategies can help us overcome limiting beliefs, manage our emotions, and develop empowering habits.

One of the key principles of NLP is that our subjective experience of the world is shaped by our internal representations. These representations are made up of our thoughts, beliefs, values, and memories. By becoming aware of these internal representations and learning to change them, we can transform our perception of reality and create new possibilities for ourselves.

Transforming Your Mindset

NLP provides a range of techniques to help you transform your mindset and achieve success. One such technique is reframing, which involves changing the way you perceive a situation by looking at it from a different perspective. By reframing limiting beliefs and negative experiences, you can shift your mindset and open yourself up to new opportunities.

Another powerful technique in NLP is visualization and mental rehearsal. By vividly imagining yourself achieving your goals and rehearsing the steps to get there, you can program your mind for success. This technique helps you build confidence, overcome obstacles, and stay focused on your desired outcomes.

Enhancing Communication Skills

Effective communication is essential for success in both personal and professional relationships. NLP offers a range of tools and techniques to enhance your communication skills and build rapport with others. One such tool is the art of rapport, which involves establishing a deep connection with others by matching their body language, tone of voice, and language patterns. By building rapport, you can create trust and understanding, and improve your ability to influence and persuade others.

Active listening is another important skill in communication, and NLP provides techniques to help you become a better listener. By fully engaging with others and understanding their perspective, you can improve your relationships and resolve conflicts more effectively.

Achieving Success in Business

NLP can also be a valuable tool for success in the business world. Leadership and influence are key skills for anyone in a managerial or leadership position. NLP techniques can help you develop these skills by understanding and modeling the behaviors of successful leaders. By studying their strategies and adopting their mindset, you can enhance your own leadership abilities and inspire others to achieve their best.

Effective decision making is another crucial skill in business. NLP provides techniques to help you make better decisions by accessing your unconscious mind and aligning your values and beliefs with your goals. By using these techniques, you can make decisions with confidence and clarity.

Negotiation and conflict resolution are also important skills in the business world. NLP offers strategies to help you understand and influence the motivations and behaviors of others, leading to more successful negotiations and resolutions.

Improving Health and Wellness

NLP can also have a positive impact on your health and wellness. The mind-body connection is a central concept in NLP, and by understanding and working with this connection, you can improve your overall well-being. NLP techniques can help you overcome bad habits, manage stress, and create a positive mindset.

By reframing your beliefs and perceptions about health and wellness, you can develop empowering habits and make healthier choices. NLP techniques can also help you manage stress by changing your response to stressful situations and developing effective coping mechanisms.

Building Strong Relationships

Relationships are a fundamental aspect of our lives, and NLP can help us build and maintain strong and fulfilling relationships. By understanding relationship dynamics and effective communication techniques, you can improve your relationships with family, friends, and romantic partners.

NLP provides strategies for resolving conflicts and building trust and intimacy. By understanding the underlying motivations and needs of others, you can navigate conflicts more effectively and build deeper connections.

Taking NLP to the Next Level

Once you have mastered the foundational principles and techniques of NLP, you can take your skills to the next level. Regression is a powerful technique in NLP that allows you to release negative emotions and limiting beliefs from your past. By working with your past, you can create a compelling future and align your actions with your goals.

Modeling excellence is another advanced technique in NLP that involves studying and replicating the behaviors and strategies of successful individuals. By modeling excellence, you can accelerate your own learning and achieve success in your chosen field.

NLP can also be applied in coaching and therapy settings. By using NLP techniques, coaches and therapists can help their clients overcome limiting beliefs, manage their emotions, and achieve their goals.

In conclusion, NLP has the potential to transform your life and career. By understanding and applying the principles and techniques of NLP, you can enhance your communication skills, develop a positive mindset, build strong relationships, and achieve success in all areas of your life. Whether you are looking to advance in your career, improve your health and wellness, or enhance your personal development, NLP provides a powerful framework for growth and transformation.

THE MINDTECH INSTITUTE

Now, you can become a fully qualified Hypnotherapist, NLP Master Practitioner, Master Life Coach, Counsellor and more by simply studying online. More accredited Diplomas (Associate Degrees) and other courses are also available at www.themindtechinstitute.com

www.mti.edu.au

CHAPTER TWO

BUILDING A STRONG FOUNDATION

Building a strong foundation in Neuro-Linguistic Programming (NLP) involves mastering fundamental principles and techniques. This includes understanding the role of language, the mind-body connection, and effective communication strategies. By honing these skills, individuals can unlock the full potential of NLP, facilitating personal growth and improved relationships.

The Power of Language

Language is a fundamental aspect of human communication and interaction. It is through language that we express our thoughts, emotions, and desires. But what if I told you that language is not just a tool for communication, but also a powerful force that can shape our reality and influence our success in life and career? This is where Neuro-Linguistic Programming (NLP) comes into play.

NLP recognizes the immense power of language and how it can impact our thoughts, beliefs, and behaviors. By understanding and harnessing the power of language, we can unlock our potential and achieve success in various aspects of our lives.

One of the key principles of NLP is that the words we use have a profound impact on our thoughts and actions. Our language not only reflects our internal experiences but also shapes them. By becoming aware of the language we use, we can gain insight into our thought patterns and beliefs, and ultimately, take control of our lives.

NLP teaches us to pay attention to the words we use when

communicating with ourselves and others. It encourages us to use language that is positive, empowering, and solution-oriented. By reframing our language, we can shift our perspective and create new possibilities for ourselves.

For example, instead of saying, "I can't do it," we can reframe it as, "I haven't figured it out yet." This simple shift in language opens up the possibility of finding a solution and encourages a growth mindset. By using language that focuses on possibilities and solutions, we can overcome challenges and achieve our goals.

Another powerful aspect of language in NLP is the use of metaphors. Metaphors are a way of communicating complex ideas and concepts in a simple and relatable manner. They tap into the power of storytelling and engage our subconscious mind, making it easier for us to understand and internalize new ideas.

Metaphors can be used to reframe our experiences and beliefs. For example, if someone sees themselves as a "failure," they can reframe it as a "learner." By using the metaphor of a learner, they can shift their perspective and see failures as opportunities for growth and learning.

In addition to the words we use, NLP also emphasizes the importance of non-verbal communication. Our body language, facial expressions, and tone of voice can convey powerful messages that go beyond the words we speak. By becoming aware of our non-verbal cues and learning to read the non-verbal cues of others, we can enhance our communication skills and build stronger connections with others.

NLP also teaches us the art of active listening. Active listening involves not only hearing the words someone is saying but also paying attention to their tone, body language, and emotions. By actively listening, we can better understand others, build rapport, and respond in a way that meets their needs.

Furthermore, NLP introduces us to the concept of persuasive language patterns. These patterns are linguistic techniques that can influence and persuade others. By understanding and using these patterns ethically, we can enhance our communication skills and effectively convey our ideas and desires.

For example, there's an excellent NLP sales technique we often teach At The MindTech Institute NLP Practitioner level is using the "chunking up" (the big picture) pattern, which involves moving from specific details to broader concepts. This can be useful when trying to convince someone of the importance or value of an idea or product. On the other hand, the "chunking down" (the small picture) pattern involves moving from broader concepts to specific details. This can be helpful when providing instructions or explaining complex ideas.

By mastering the power of language through NLP, we can transform our communication skills and enhance our personal and professional relationships. We can become more effective leaders, negotiators, and influencers. We can build trust, resolve conflicts, and create a positive and supportive environment.

In conclusion, language is a powerful tool that can shape our reality and influence our success in life and career. By understanding and harnessing the power of language through NLP, we can unlock our potential and achieve our goals. Whether it's building strong relationships, excelling in business, or mastering self, the power of language is a key component of our journey towards success.

The Map is Not the Territory

In the world of Neuro-Linguistic Programming (NLP), there is a fundamental concept that holds great significance: "The map is not the territory." This simple yet profound idea forms the basis of understanding how our perceptions and interpretations of the world shape our experiences and interactions.

Imagine you are planning a trip to a new city. Before embarking on your journey, you study a map to familiarize yourself with the streets, landmarks, and attractions. The map serves as a representation of the city, providing you with a guide to navigate and explore. However, it is important to remember that the map is not the actual city itself. It is merely a representation, a simplified version of the real thing.

Similarly, in NLP, the map refers to our subjective experience of the world. It encompasses our beliefs, values, thoughts, and perceptions. It is the lens through which we interpret and make sense of our experiences. However, it is crucial to recognize that our map is not an accurate reflection of reality. It is a filtered and subjective representation.

Understanding this concept is essential because it allows us to recognize that our perceptions may not always align with objective reality. Our map is influenced by our past experiences, cultural conditioning, beliefs, and biases. It is shaped by our unique set of filters, which include our senses, language, memories, and emotions. As a result, our map may differ from someone else's map, leading to different interpretations and understandings of the same situation.

By acknowledging that the map is not the territory, we open ourselves up to new possibilities and perspectives. We become aware that our map is not fixed or absolute, but rather a malleable and changeable construct. This realization empowers us to question our assumptions, challenge our limiting beliefs, and explore alternative viewpoints.

In the context of personal and professional development, understanding that the map is not the territory allows us to break free from self-imposed limitations. Often, we create mental barriers and constraints based on our subjective interpretations of the world. We may hold limiting beliefs about our abilities, potential, or worthiness of success. These beliefs act as filters that shape our thoughts, emotions, and behaviors, ultimately influencing our outcomes.

NLP provides us with tools and techniques to examine and modify our maps. Through various processes such as reframing, anchoring, and modeling excellence, we can reshape our perceptions and create more empowering maps. We can challenge and reframe limiting beliefs, replacing them with more empowering ones that support our growth and success.

For example, let's say you have a belief that you are not good enough to pursue your dream career. This belief acts as a filter, distorting your perception of your abilities and potential. Through NLP techniques, you can reframe this belief by examining the evidence that supports it and challenging its validity. You can explore alternative perspectives and gather evidence that contradicts your limiting belief. By doing so, you can create a new map that aligns with your true capabilities and aspirations.

Furthermore, understanding that the map is not the territory enhances our communication and relationships. We recognize that each person has their own unique map, shaped by their experiences, beliefs, and values. This awareness allows us to approach interactions with empathy, curiosity, and open-mindedness. We can seek to understand the other person's map, rather than assuming that our map is the only valid one.

In the realm of business and leadership, recognizing that the map is not the territory is crucial for effective decision-making and problem-solving. It encourages us to consider multiple perspectives, gather diverse input, and challenge our assumptions. By doing so, we can make more informed and inclusive decisions that take into account the complexity and diversity of the real world.

In summary, the concept of "The map is not the territory" is a foundational principle in Neuro-Linguistic Programming. It reminds us that our subjective experience of the world is not an accurate representation of reality. By understanding this, we can challenge our limiting beliefs, reshape our perceptions, and enhance our communication and relationships. Embracing this concept empowers us to unlock our potential and harness the power of NLP for success in life and career.

Anchoring

Anchoring is a powerful technique in Neuro-Linguistic Programming (NLP) that allows you to create and access specific states of mind and emotions at will. Just like a physical anchor holds a ship in place, an NLP anchor is a trigger that can be used to evoke a desired state or emotion. By consciously creating and utilizing anchors, you can enhance your ability to achieve success, overcome challenges, and improve your overall well-being.

Understanding Anchoring

Anchoring is based on the principle that our experiences are associated with specific internal and external stimuli. These stimuli can be anything from a touch, a sound, a smell, or even a specific word or phrase. When we experience a particular state or emotion in conjunction with a specific stimulus, our mind forms an unconscious connection between the two. This connection becomes an anchor that can be activated in the future to access the associated state or emotion.

For example, think about a time when you felt incredibly confident and empowered. Perhaps it was during a successful presentation or when you achieved a significant goal. Now, try to recall the specific physical sensations, thoughts, and emotions you experienced in that moment. By consciously associating those sensations with a unique gesture, such as touching your thumb and index finger together, you can create an anchor for confidence and empowerment.

Creating Anchors

During the NLP Practitioner and Master Practitioner levels workshop or online course at The MindTech Institute we teach advanced anchoring in more details. However, basically to create an anchor, follow these steps:

Choose a specific state or emotion you want to anchor. It could be confidence, motivation, relaxation, or any other desired state.

Recall a time when you experienced that state or emotion vividly. Remember the specific details of that experience, including the physical sensations, thoughts, and emotions associated with it.

Choose a unique and consistent stimulus to associate with the desired state. This could be a touch, a word, a sound, or even a visualization.

As you vividly recall the desired state, apply the chosen stimulus at its peak intensity. For example, if you want to anchor confidence, touch your thumb and index finger together at the moment when you feel the most confident.

Repeat this process several times to strengthen the association between the stimulus and the desired state. Each time you apply the stimulus, intensify the state by making it more vivid and intense.

Accessing Anchors

Once you have created an anchor, you can use it to access the desired state or emotion whenever you need it. To activate an anchor, follow these steps:

Relax and clear your mind. Take a few deep breaths to center yourself.

Physically apply the stimulus associated with the anchor. For example, touch your thumb and index finger together if that was the chosen stimulus.

As you apply the stimulus, vividly recall the experience when you first created the anchor. Remember the physical sensations, thoughts, and emotions associated with the desired state.

Allow yourself to fully immerse in the desired state or emotion. Feel it in your body, hear the empowering thoughts, and experience the positive emotions.

By consistently practicing and reinforcing your anchors, you can strengthen their effectiveness and make them more readily accessible. Over time, the mere application of the stimulus will be enough to evoke the desired state or emotion, allowing you to tap into your inner resources whenever you need them.

Utilizing Anchors for Success

Anchoring can be a valuable tool for achieving success in various areas of your life. Here are some ways you can utilize anchors to enhance your personal and professional development:

1. Boosting Confidence and Motivation

Create anchors for confidence and motivation to help you overcome self-doubt and procrastination. By associating these empowering states with specific stimuli, you can quickly shift your mindset and tap into your inner drive whenever you need a boost.

2. Managing Stress and Anxiety

Anchors can be used to manage stress and anxiety by creating a sense of calm and relaxation. By associating a specific stimulus with a state of tranquility, you can activate the anchor during stressful situations to help you stay centered and focused.

3. Enhancing Performance

Anchors can be utilized to enhance performance in various areas, such as public speaking, sports, or creative endeavors. By creating anchors for peak performance states, you can access them at will, allowing you to perform at your best when it matters most.

4. Overcoming Limiting Beliefs

Anchors can also be used to overcome limiting beliefs and negative thought patterns. By associating empowering states with specific stimuli, you can interrupt negative thought loops and replace them with more positive and empowering beliefs.

5. Improving Communication and Relationships

Anchoring can be applied to improve communication and build stronger relationships. By creating anchors for rapport, empathy, and understanding, you can establish deeper connections with others and enhance your ability to communicate effectively.

6. Managing Emotional States

Anchors can help you manage and shift your emotional states. By creating anchors for states such as joy, gratitude, or resilience, you can quickly shift from negative emotions to more positive and resourceful states.

Anchoring is a powerful technique in Neuro-Linguistic Programming that allows you to access desired states and emotions at will. By consciously creating and utilizing anchors, you can enhance your personal and professional development, improve your communication skills, and achieve greater success in all areas of your life. Practice and refine your anchors regularly to strengthen their effectiveness and unlock your full potential.

Modeling Excellence

In the world of Neuro-Linguistic Programming (NLP), one of the most powerful techniques is known as modeling excellence. This technique involves studying and replicating the behaviors, beliefs, and strategies of individuals who have achieved outstanding success in a particular area of life. By understanding and adopting their mindset and actions, you can unlock your own potential and achieve similar levels of excellence.

Modeling excellence is based on the belief that success leaves clues. By observing and analyzing the patterns and strategies of successful individuals, you can uncover the underlying principles that contribute to their achievements. This process allows you to replicate their success in your own life, whether it be in your career, relationships, health, or personal development.

To begin the process of modeling excellence, it is important to identify someone who has achieved the level of success you desire in a specific area. This could be a renowned entrepreneur, a top athlete, a successful artist, or even a great leader. The key is to choose someone who embodies the qualities and skills you wish to develop within yourself.

Once you have identified your role model, the next step is to study and analyze their behaviors, beliefs, and strategies. This can be done through various means, such as reading their biographies, watching interviews or documentaries about them, or even directly interacting with them if possible. The goal is to gain a deep understanding of how they think, what actions they take, and the mindset they possess.

During the process of modeling, it is important to pay attention to both the conscious and unconscious aspects of your role model's behavior. This includes their language patterns, body language, decision-making processes, and the beliefs they hold about themselves and the world. By studying these aspects, you can begin to uncover the underlying patterns and strategies that contribute to their success.

Once you have gathered enough information about your role

model, the next step is to begin implementing their strategies and beliefs into your own life. This involves adopting their mindset, practicing their behaviors, and integrating their strategies into your daily routines. By consistently applying these principles, you can start to see positive changes and improvements in your own life.

It is important to note that modeling excellence is not about blindly copying someone else's actions. It is about understanding the underlying principles and adapting them to suit your own unique circumstances and goals. By doing so, you can create your own path to success while leveraging the wisdom and strategies of those who have already achieved greatness.

Modeling excellence can be applied to various areas of life. For example, if you are looking to excel in your career, you can model the behaviors and strategies of successful individuals in your field. This could involve studying their work ethic, networking skills, problem-solving abilities, or any other qualities that contribute to their success. By adopting these qualities, you can enhance your own performance and increase your chances of achieving similar levels of success.

Similarly, modeling excellence can be applied to relationships. By studying the behaviors and communication styles of individuals who have thriving relationships, you can learn valuable insights into building trust, resolving conflicts, and fostering intimacy. By incorporating these strategies into your own relationships, you can create stronger and more fulfilling connections with others.

In summary, modeling excellence is a powerful technique within the realm of Neuro-Linguistic Programming (NLP) that allows you to replicate the success of individuals who have achieved greatness in a specific area. By studying their behaviors, beliefs, and strategies, you can uncover the underlying principles that contribute to their success and apply them to your own life. Whether it be in your career, relationships, health, or personal development, modeling excellence can unlock your potential and propel you towards achieving your goals.

THE MINDTECH
INSTITUTE

Now, you can become a fully qualified Hypnotherapist, NLP Master Practitioner, Master Life Coach, Counsellor and more by simply studying online. More accredited Diplomas (Associate Degrees) and other courses are also available at www.themindtechinstitute.com

www.mti.edu.au

CHAPTER THREE
MASTERING SELF

Mastering oneself through Neuro-Linguistic Programming (NLP) involves harnessing techniques to enhance self-awareness, control emotions, and achieve personal goals. NLP empowers individuals to reprogram limiting beliefs, develop effective habits, and foster a positive mindset, leading to greater self-confidence and success in various aspects of life.

Setting Compelling Goals

Setting goals is an essential step in achieving success in any area of life. Without clear and compelling goals, we can easily find ourselves drifting aimlessly, lacking direction and purpose. Neuro-Linguistic Programming (NLP) offers powerful techniques and strategies for setting and achieving goals that can transform your life and career.

The Power of Goal Setting

Goals provide us with a sense of purpose and direction. They give us something to strive for and motivate us to take action. When we set goals, we are essentially creating a roadmap for our desired future. Without goals, we may find ourselves stuck in a cycle of mediocrity, never fully realizing our true potential.

Setting compelling goals is about more than just writing down a list of things we want to achieve. It involves tapping into our deepest desires and aligning our actions with our values and passions. When we set goals that are meaningful and inspiring to us, we are more likely to stay committed and motivated, even when faced with challenges and setbacks.

The NLP Approach to Goal Setting

Neuro-Linguistic Programming offers a unique approach to goal setting that goes beyond traditional methods. NLP recognizes that our thoughts, beliefs, and language play a crucial role in shaping our reality. By harnessing the power of our mind and language, we can create a compelling vision of our desired future and program our subconscious mind for success.

One of the key principles of NLP goal setting is to make our goals specific and measurable. Vague and general goals are less likely to be achieved because they lack clarity and focus. By clearly defining what we want to achieve and setting measurable targets, we increase our chances of success.

Another important aspect of NLP goal setting is to make our goals realistic and achievable. While it's important to dream big and aim high, setting unrealistic goals can lead to frustration and disappointment. By setting goals that are within our reach, we build confidence and momentum as we achieve smaller milestones along the way.

NLP also emphasizes the importance of setting goals that are aligned with our values and beliefs. When our goals are in harmony with our core values, we are more likely to stay motivated and committed. NLP techniques such as values elicitation can help us uncover our deepest values and ensure that our goals are in alignment with them.

The NLP Goal Setting Process

The NLP goal setting process involves several steps that help us clarify our goals and create a roadmap for their achievement. Here is a step-by-step guide to setting compelling goals using NLP techniques:

Identify Your Outcome: Begin by clearly defining what you want to achieve. Be specific and use sensory-based language to create a vivid picture of your desired outcome. For example, instead of saying "I want to lose weight," you could say "I want to weigh 150 pounds and feel healthy and energized." Also, from an NLP point of view, the word losing is a negative word that the subconscious mind tends to steer away from. Hence, most people when they "lose" weight tend to put the weight back because they have lost something (yo-yo diet). When we lose something the subconscious mind tends to find it and bring it back. Therefore, in NLP we use the phrase "get rid of unnecessary weight" rather than losing. We also reframe the word "diet" with "healthy eating" because the word diet includes "die" in it which is also not recommended on the subconscious level. That's the power of words that most people don't realize how to use resulting in failure to achieve their goals.

Make it Measurable: Break down your outcome into specific, measurable targets. This allows you to track your progress and stay motivated. For example, if your outcome is to start a successful business, you could set targets such as "I will generate $10,000 in revenue in the first six months."

Check for Ecology: Consider the impact of your goals on other areas of your life. Ensure that your goals are in alignment with your values and beliefs and that they do not conflict with other important areas of your life.

Chunk Down: Break your goals down into smaller, manageable steps. This makes them less overwhelming and increases your chances of success. For example, if your goal is to run a marathon, you could start by running a mile, then gradually increase your distance over time.

Create a Compelling Vision: Goals must always be positive in order for the subconscious mind to accept them and to help you to achieve them. Use visualization techniques to create a compelling mental image of your desired outcome. Imagine yourself already achieving your goal and experience the emotions associated with it. This helps program your subconscious mind for success.

Take Action: Finally, take consistent action towards your goals. Break your action steps into daily or weekly tasks and commit to following through. Regularly review your progress and make any necessary adjustments along the way.

By following this NLP goal setting process, you can set compelling goals that inspire and motivate you to take action. Remember, the key to achieving your goals is not just in the setting, but in the consistent and focused action you take towards them.

Setting compelling goals is a fundamental step in unlocking your potential and achieving success in life and career. Neuro-Linguistic Programming provides powerful techniques and strategies for setting and achieving goals that go beyond traditional methods. By harnessing the power of your mind and language, you can create a clear vision of your desired future and program your subconscious mind for success. Take the time to set compelling goals that are aligned with your values and passions, and commit to taking consistent action towards them. With NLP, you have the tools to unlock your potential and create the life and career you truly desire.

Reframing Limiting Beliefs

In our journey towards unlocking our potential and achieving success in life and career, one of the most important aspects to address is our beliefs. Our beliefs shape our thoughts, emotions, and actions, and ultimately determine the outcomes we experience. However, not all beliefs serve us well. In fact, many of us hold onto limiting beliefs that hold us back from reaching our full potential. These limiting beliefs act as barriers, preventing us from taking risks, pursuing our dreams, and achieving the success we desire.

But what exactly are limiting beliefs? Limiting beliefs are negative thoughts or perceptions that we hold about ourselves, others, or the world around us. They are often deeply ingrained and can stem from past experiences, societal conditioning, or even self-doubt. These beliefs create a fixed mindset, where we believe that our abilities, talents, and potential are limited. As a result, we may find ourselves stuck in a cycle of self-sabotage, fear, and missed opportunities.

The good news is that with the power of Neuro-Linguistic Programming (NLP), we can reframe these limiting beliefs and replace them with empowering ones. Reframing is a technique used in NLP that involves changing the way we perceive and interpret our experiences. By reframing our beliefs, we can shift our mindset from one of limitation to one of possibility and abundance.

So how do we go about reframing our limiting beliefs? Here are some steps to help you get started:

Identify your limiting beliefs: The first step in reframing your limiting beliefs is to become aware of them. Take some time to reflect on the thoughts and beliefs that hold you back. What do you tell yourself when faced with a challenge or opportunity? Are there any recurring negative thoughts or self-doubt that you experience? Write down these beliefs and acknowledge their presence in your life.

Challenge the validity of your beliefs: Once you have

identified your limiting beliefs, it's important to question their validity. Ask yourself whether these beliefs are based on facts or simply assumptions. Are there any past experiences or evidence that support or contradict these beliefs? Often, we hold onto beliefs that are not grounded in reality, and by challenging them, we can begin to see them for what they truly are - limitations that can be overcome.

Find evidence to support empowering beliefs: Reframing involves replacing limiting beliefs with empowering ones. To do this, you need to find evidence that supports your new beliefs. Look for examples of people who have achieved what you aspire to achieve, despite facing similar challenges or setbacks. Surround yourself with positive role models and success stories that inspire you to believe in your own potential.

Change your language and self-talk: The words we use have a powerful impact on our beliefs and mindset. Start using positive and empowering language when talking to yourself and others. Instead of saying "I can't do it," say "I am capable of overcoming any challenge." By changing your language, you can begin to rewire your brain and reinforce your new empowering beliefs.

Visualize success: Visualization is a powerful tool in reframing limiting beliefs. Take some time each day to visualize yourself achieving your goals and living the life you desire. See yourself overcoming obstacles, feeling confident, and experiencing success. By repeatedly visualizing these positive outcomes, you can reprogram your subconscious mind and align it with your new empowering beliefs.

Take action and challenge your comfort zone: Reframing your limiting beliefs is not just about changing your thoughts; it's also about taking action. Challenge yourself to step outside of your comfort zone and take small steps towards your goals. Each time you take action, you prove to yourself that your new empowering beliefs are true and achievable.

Remember, reframing limiting beliefs is a process that takes time and practice. Be patient with yourself and celebrate each small victory along the way. As you continue to reframe your beliefs, you will notice a shift in your mindset, confidence, and ability to achieve success in all areas of your life.

By harnessing the power of NLP and reframing your limiting beliefs, you can unlock your true potential and create a life filled with success, happiness, and fulfillment. So, start today and embrace the journey of transformation and growth.

Managing Emotions

Emotions play a significant role in our lives. They can either propel us forward or hold us back from achieving our goals and living a fulfilling life. In this section, we will explore how Neuro-Linguistic Programming (NLP) can help you effectively manage your emotions and harness their power to create positive change in your life.

Understanding Emotions

Before we delve into managing emotions, it is essential to understand what emotions are and how they influence our thoughts, behaviors, and overall well-being. Emotions are complex physiological and psychological responses to external or internal stimuli. They can range from joy and excitement to fear and sadness.

NLP teaches us that emotions are not inherently good or bad; they are simply signals that provide us with valuable information about our experiences and perceptions. By understanding and managing our emotions, we can gain greater control over our thoughts and actions, leading to improved decision-making and overall emotional well-being.

The NLP Approach to Managing Emotions

NLP offers a range of techniques and strategies to help individuals effectively manage their emotions. These techniques are designed to help you gain awareness of your emotional states, understand the underlying patterns and triggers, and ultimately shift your emotional responses in a more positive and empowering direction.

1. Anchoring: Anchoring is a powerful NLP technique that allows you to associate a specific emotional state with a particular trigger or stimulus. By consciously creating and anchoring positive emotions to specific triggers, you can access those emotions whenever you need them.

For example, if you want to feel confident before a presentation, you can anchor that feeling by associating it with a physical gesture, such as touching your thumb and index finger together. Over time, by consistently anchoring confidence to this gesture, you can access that state of confidence whenever you perform the gesture.

2. Reframing: Reframing is another valuable NLP technique that involves changing the meaning or perspective of a situation or experience. By reframing negative or disempowering emotions, you can transform them into positive and empowering ones.

For instance, if you find yourself feeling anxious about a job interview, you can reframe that anxiety as excitement and anticipation. By shifting your perspective, you can channel that energy into a positive and productive mindset, enhancing your performance during the interview. Keep in mind that anxiety and excitement produce many of the same neurological responses. And so, switching between the two can just be a matter of thinking positively or negatively.

3. Submodalities: Submodalities refer to the sensory qualities of our internal representations. In NLP, we can use submodalities to change the way we experience and respond to emotions. By altering the submodalities associated with a particular emotion, we can change its intensity and impact on our lives.

For example, if you tend to experience fear as a vivid and overwhelming image in your mind, you can use NLP techniques to change the submodalities of that image. By making it smaller, dimmer, or even black and white, you can reduce the intensity of the fear and gain greater control over your emotional response.

4. Anchoring Resourceful States: In addition to anchoring positive emotions, NLP also allows you to anchor resourceful states. Resourceful states are emotional states that empower you and enable you to perform at your best. By anchoring these resourceful states, you can access them whenever you need to overcome challenges or achieve your goals.

For example, if you want to feel motivated and focused before starting a new project, you can anchor that state by associating it with a specific gesture or word. By consistently anchoring this resourceful state, you can tap into it whenever you need a boost of motivation and focus.

5. Regression Therapy: Regression Therapy is now a part of our Hypnosis Training at The MindTech Institute. It's simply a powerful technique that involves working with the concept of time to release negative emotions and limiting beliefs. By revisiting past experiences and reframing them from a more empowering perspective, you can let go of emotional baggage and create a more positive future.

Through the Regression Therapy, you can also set compelling goals and create a clear vision of your desired future. By aligning your emotions with your goals, you can enhance your motivation and drive to achieve them.

Integrating NLP Techniques into Your Life

To effectively manage your emotions using NLP techniques, it is essential to integrate them into your daily life. Here are some practical steps you can take:

Practice self-awareness: Pay attention to your emotions and the triggers that elicit them. Notice any patterns or recurring themes.

Apply anchoring: Identify the emotions you want to anchor and choose a physical gesture or trigger to associate with them. Practice anchoring these emotions regularly to strengthen the association.

Reframe negative emotions: When you experience negative emotions, consciously reframe them by changing your perspective or finding a more empowering meaning.

Experiment with submodalities: Explore the sensory qualities of your emotions and experiment with altering them to change your emotional responses.

Anchor resourceful states: Identify the resourceful states that empower you and anchor them to specific triggers or gestures. Practice accessing these states whenever you need them.

Consider Regression Therapy: If you have unresolved emotional issues or limiting beliefs, consider contacting The MindTech Institute seeking professional assistance to work through them using Regression Therapy.

By consistently applying these techniques and integrating them into your daily life, you can effectively manage your emotions and harness their power to create positive change in all areas of your life.

In the next section, we will explore the importance of creating empowering habits and how NLP can help you develop habits that support your success and well-being.

Creating Empowering Habits

Habits are the building blocks of our lives. They shape our actions, behaviors, and ultimately, our outcomes. In the realm of Neuro-Linguistic Programming (NLP), creating empowering habits is a fundamental aspect of personal and professional growth. By understanding the power of habits and utilizing NLP techniques, you can transform your life and career in remarkable ways.

The Power of Habits

Habits are deeply ingrained patterns of behavior that we perform automatically, often without conscious thought. They can either propel us forward or hold us back, depending on whether they are empowering or limiting. Our habits are formed through repetition and reinforcement, and they have a profound impact on our daily lives.

NLP recognizes the significance of habits and provides tools and techniques to help us create empowering habits that align with our goals and aspirations. By consciously designing our habits, we can shape our actions and behaviors in a way that supports our personal and professional growth.

The Habit Loop

To understand how to create empowering habits, it is essential to grasp the concept of the habit loop. The habit loop consists of three components: the cue, the routine, and the reward. Understanding this loop allows us to identify and modify our existing habits or create new ones.

Cue: The cue is the trigger that initiates the habit. It can be a specific time of day, a particular location, an emotional state, or even the presence of certain people. By identifying the cues that prompt our habits, we can gain insight into the underlying motivations and triggers.

Routine: The routine is the actual behavior or action that follows the cue. It is the habit itself. For example, if the cue is feeling stressed, the routine might be reaching for a sugary snack. By examining our routines, we can determine whether they are empowering or limiting.

Reward: The reward is the positive reinforcement that follows the routine. It is what motivates us to repeat the habit. In the case of the sugary snack, the reward might be a temporary boost in mood or energy. By understanding the rewards we seek, we can find alternative, healthier ways to satisfy those needs.

Utilizing NLP Techniques for Habit Creation

NLP offers a range of techniques that can be applied to create empowering habits and break free from limiting ones. Here are some powerful strategies to help you harness the power of NLP in habit formation:

1. Anchoring: Anchoring is a technique that allows you to associate a specific state of mind or emotion with a physical or sensory stimulus. By anchoring positive emotions to a specific action or cue, you can create a habit that reinforces those emotions. For example, if you want to cultivate a habit of confidence before a presentation, you can anchor the feeling of confidence to a specific gesture or phrase.

2. Reframing: Reframing is a technique that involves changing the way we perceive a situation or experience. By reframing our thoughts and beliefs about a habit, we can transform it from a limiting behavior to an empowering one. For example, if you have a habit of procrastination, you can reframe it as a habit of taking deliberate breaks to recharge your energy.

3. Visualization and Mental Rehearsal: Visualization and mental rehearsal are powerful techniques that allow you to create a vivid mental image of yourself engaging in the desired habit. By repeatedly visualizing yourself successfully performing the habit, you strengthen the neural pathways associated with that behavior. This technique enhances your motivation and increases the likelihood of successfully adopting the habit.

4. Building on Existing Habits: Another effective strategy is to build new habits on top of existing ones. By piggybacking a new habit onto an existing routine, you leverage the power of habit stacking. For example, if you already have a habit of brushing your teeth before bed, you can add the habit of reading for 10 minutes immediately after brushing.

5. Setting SMART Goals: Setting Specific, Measurable, Achievable, Relevant, and Time-bound (SMART) goals is crucial for habit formation. By clearly defining what you want to achieve and setting a timeline, you create a roadmap for success. SMART goals provide clarity and focus, making it easier to track your progress and stay motivated.

6. Creating a Supportive Environment: Surrounding yourself with a supportive environment can significantly impact your ability to create empowering habits. This includes both physical and social environments. Arrange your physical space in a way that supports your desired habits, and seek out like-minded individuals who can provide encouragement and accountability.

The Compound Effect of Empowering Habits

Creating empowering habits is not a one-time event but an ongoing process. It requires consistency, commitment, and a growth mindset. However, the rewards of cultivating empowering habits are immense.

Empowering habits have a compound effect on our lives. They create a positive ripple effect, influencing other areas of our personal and professional lives. When we consistently engage in empowering habits, we build momentum and increase our chances of success. These habits become the foundation upon which we can achieve our goals, improve our relationships, enhance our communication skills, and excel in our careers.

By utilizing the power of NLP techniques and consciously designing our habits, we unlock our potential and create a life of fulfillment and success. Remember, it is the small, consistent actions that lead to significant transformations. Start today by identifying the habits you want to create, apply the NLP techniques discussed in this section, and watch as your life and career flourish.

Visualization and Mental Rehearsal

Visualization and mental rehearsal are powerful techniques used in Neuro-Linguistic Programming (NLP) to enhance performance, achieve goals, and create positive outcomes. By harnessing the power of the mind, individuals can create vivid mental images and rehearse desired outcomes, effectively programming their subconscious mind for success.

The Power of Visualization

Visualization is the process of creating detailed mental images of desired outcomes or goals. It involves using all the senses to make the visualization as vivid and real as possible. When we visualize, we activate the same neural pathways in our brain as when we actually experience the event, creating a powerful connection between our thoughts and our actions.

Visualization allows us to tap into the power of our imagination and create a clear picture of what we want to achieve. By repeatedly visualizing our goals, we send a clear message to our subconscious mind about what we want to manifest in our lives. This helps to align our thoughts, beliefs, and actions with our desired outcomes, increasing the likelihood of success.

The Process of Visualization

To effectively use visualization, follow these steps:

Set Clear Goals: Before you begin visualizing, it's important to have a clear understanding of what you want to achieve. Set specific, measurable, achievable, relevant, and time-bound (SMART) goals that are aligned with your values and aspirations.

Create a Relaxing Environment: Find a quiet and comfortable space where you can relax and focus without distractions. Close your eyes and take a few deep breaths to calm your mind and body.

Visualize in Detail: Begin by visualizing your desired outcome in as much detail as possible. Imagine yourself in the situation, experiencing it with all your senses. See the colors, hear the sounds, feel the textures, and even taste the sensations if applicable. Make the visualization as vivid and real as you can.

Engage Your Emotions: As you visualize, engage your emotions and feel the positive emotions associated with achieving your goal. Whether it's excitement, joy, or a sense of accomplishment, allow yourself to fully experience these emotions as if the goal has already been achieved.

Rehearse the Process: In addition to visualizing the end result, also visualize the steps you need to take to achieve your goal. Imagine yourself taking action, overcoming obstacles, and successfully navigating the journey towards your desired outcome. This mental rehearsal helps to build confidence and prepares your mind for success.

Repeat Regularly: Consistency is key when it comes to visualization. Set aside dedicated time each day to practice visualization. The more you repeat the process, the more your subconscious mind will accept the visualized outcome as reality, increasing the likelihood of it manifesting in your life.

The Benefits of Visualization

Visualization offers numerous benefits for personal and professional development. Here are some of the key advantages:

Enhanced Performance: Visualization helps to improve performance by programming the mind for success. Athletes, for example, use visualization techniques to mentally rehearse their performances, enhancing their skills and boosting their confidence.

Goal Achievement: By consistently visualizing your goals, you create a clear roadmap for success. Visualization aligns your thoughts, beliefs, and actions with your desired outcomes, increasing your motivation and focus to achieve them.

Increased Confidence: Visualization builds confidence by allowing you to see yourself succeeding. As you repeatedly visualize positive outcomes, your subconscious mind begins to accept them as reality, boosting your self-belief and confidence.

Stress Reduction: Visualization can be a powerful tool for managing stress and anxiety. By visualizing calm and peaceful scenarios, you can activate the relaxation response in your body, reducing stress levels and promoting overall well-being.

Improved Creativity: Visualization stimulates the creative centers of the brain, allowing you to generate new ideas and solutions. By visualizing different scenarios and possibilities, you can expand your thinking and tap into your creative potential.

Positive Mindset: Visualization helps to cultivate a positive mindset by focusing on desired outcomes and possibilities. By consistently visualizing positive experiences, you rewire your brain to seek out and create more positive experiences in your life.

Tips for Effective Visualization

To make the most of visualization, consider the following tips:

Be Specific: Clearly define your goals and visualize them in specific detail. The more specific you are, the more powerful the visualization becomes.

Engage All Senses: Use all your senses to make the visualization as vivid and real as possible. Engaging all senses strengthens the neural connections in your brain and enhances the effectiveness of the visualization.

Believe in the Outcome: Approach visualization with a sense of belief and certainty. Trust that your goals are achievable and that the visualization process will help you manifest them.

Practice Regularly: Consistency is key. Set aside dedicated time each day to practice visualization. The more you practice, the more effective it becomes.

Combine with Action: Visualization is a powerful tool, but it should be complemented with action. Take inspired action towards your goals and use visualization to enhance your performance and mindset along the way.

Visualization and mental rehearsal are valuable tools in unlocking your potential and achieving success in all areas of life. By harnessing the power of your mind and consistently visualizing your goals, you can program your subconscious mind for success, enhance your performance, and create the life you desire.

Building Confidence and Self-Esteem

Confidence and self-esteem are essential components of personal and professional success. They shape our beliefs about ourselves and influence how we interact with the world around us. Neuro-Linguistic Programming (NLP) offers powerful techniques and strategies to help individuals build and enhance their confidence and self-esteem.

Understanding Confidence and Self-Esteem

Confidence refers to the belief in one's abilities, skills, and knowledge. It is the inner assurance that allows individuals to take risks, face challenges, and overcome obstacles. Self-esteem, on the other hand, is the overall evaluation and perception of one's worth and value as a person. It encompasses how we feel about ourselves, our abilities, and our place in the world.

Confidence and self-esteem are closely intertwined. When we have high self-esteem, we tend to have greater confidence in our abilities. Conversely, low self-esteem can undermine our confidence and hinder our progress in various areas of life.

The Role of NLP in Building Confidence and Self-Esteem

NLP provides a range of techniques and strategies that can help individuals build and enhance their confidence and self-esteem. By understanding and utilizing the power of language, beliefs, and patterns of thinking, NLP empowers individuals to transform their self-perception and develop a strong sense of self-worth.

Reframing Limiting Beliefs

One of the key aspects of building confidence and self-esteem is identifying and reframing limiting beliefs. Limiting beliefs are negative thoughts or beliefs that hold us back from reaching our full potential. They often stem from past experiences, societal conditioning, or self-imposed limitations.

NLP offers powerful techniques to reframe these limiting beliefs and replace them with empowering ones. By challenging and questioning the validity of these beliefs, individuals can shift their perspective and adopt more positive and empowering beliefs about themselves and their abilities.

Anchoring Confidence

Anchoring is a technique in NLP that allows individuals to associate a specific state of mind or emotion with a physical or mental trigger. By creating an anchor for confidence, individuals can access that state of confidence whenever they need it.

To anchor confidence, individuals can recall a time when they felt exceptionally confident and fully immerse themselves in that memory. They can then create a physical anchor, such as pressing their thumb and forefinger together, to associate with that confident state. By consistently using the anchor in situations where confidence is required, individuals can access their confident state effortlessly.

Modeling Excellence

Another powerful technique in NLP for building confidence and self-esteem is modeling excellence. Modeling involves studying and emulating the behaviors, beliefs, and strategies of individuals who excel in a particular area.

By identifying someone who embodies the confidence and self-esteem they desire, individuals can study their mindset, language patterns, and behaviors. Through modeling, individuals can adopt these qualities and integrate them into their own lives, thereby enhancing their own confidence and self-esteem.

Visualization and Mental Rehearsal

Visualization and mental rehearsal are techniques used in NLP to enhance confidence and self-esteem. By vividly imagining oneself successfully performing a task or achieving a goal, individuals can create a positive mental image that boosts their confidence.

Through regular practice of visualization and mental rehearsal, individuals can strengthen their belief in their abilities and increase their self-esteem. This technique allows individuals to mentally prepare for challenging situations, reducing anxiety and increasing their chances of success.

Affirmations and Positive Self-Talk

Affirmations and positive self-talk are powerful tools in building confidence and self-esteem. By consciously choosing positive and empowering statements about oneself, individuals can reprogram their subconscious mind and reinforce positive beliefs.

NLP encourages individuals to create affirmations that are specific, positive, and in the present tense. By repeating these affirmations regularly, individuals can gradually shift their self-perception and develop a strong sense of confidence and self-worth.

Applying NLP Techniques for Building Confidence and Self-Esteem

To effectively build confidence and self-esteem using NLP techniques, it is important to practice consistency and persistence. Here are some practical steps to apply these techniques in your life:

Identify and challenge limiting beliefs: Take time to reflect on any negative beliefs that may be holding you back. Question their validity and replace them with empowering beliefs.

Create anchors for confidence: Recall a time when you felt exceptionally confident and create a physical or mental anchor to associate with that state. Practice using the anchor in situations where confidence is required.

Model excellence: Identify individuals who embody the confidence and self-esteem you desire. Study their mindset, language patterns, and behaviors, and integrate them into your own life.

Practice visualization and mental rehearsal: Regularly visualize yourself successfully performing tasks or achieving goals. Engage all your senses and create a vivid mental image of success.

Use affirmations and positive self-talk: Create positive and empowering affirmations that reflect your desired level of confidence and self-esteem. Repeat them regularly and believe in their truth.

By consistently applying these techniques, you can gradually build and enhance your confidence and self-esteem. Remember that building confidence and self-esteem is a journey, and it requires patience, practice, and self-compassion. With NLP as your guide, you have the tools to unlock your potential and cultivate a strong sense of self-worth that will propel you towards success in all areas of life.

CHAPTER FOUR

EFFECTIVE COMMUNICATION

Neuro-Linguistic Programming (NLP) equips individuals with tools for effective communication. It focuses on understanding and utilizing language patterns, non-verbal cues, and rapport-building techniques to enhance interpersonal interactions. NLP helps improve listening skills, resolve conflicts, and establish meaningful connections, fostering more persuasive and empathetic communication.

The Art of Rapport
Rapport is the foundation of effective communication and connection with others. It is the ability to establish a harmonious relationship, where trust, understanding, and mutual respect thrive. In the context of Neuro-Linguistic Programming (NLP), rapport is considered an essential skill that can greatly enhance your personal and professional interactions.

When you are in rapport with someone, you are in sync with them on multiple levels - verbal, non-verbal, and energetic. It is as if you are speaking the same language, both literally and metaphorically. Building rapport allows you to create a comfortable and conducive environment for open communication, collaboration, and influence.

The Elements of Rapport
Rapport is not just about mirroring someone's body language or

using similar words. It goes beyond surface-level mimicry and requires a deeper understanding of human communication. NLP offers several techniques and strategies to help you establish and maintain rapport effortlessly.

Matching and Mirroring: One of the fundamental techniques in building rapport is matching and mirroring the other person's physiology, voice tone, and language patterns. By subtly imitating their gestures, posture, and speech patterns, you create a sense of familiarity and connection. However, it is important to note that matching and mirroring should be done subtly and respectfully, without appearing forced or artificial.

Pacing and Leading: Pacing involves aligning yourself with the other person's communication style and pace. By matching their tempo, volume, and rhythm, you establish a sense of harmony and understanding. Once rapport is established, you can then lead the interaction by gradually introducing your own style and pace. Pacing and leading allows you to guide the conversation while maintaining rapport and cooperation.

Calibration: Calibration is the ability to observe and interpret subtle cues from the other person's verbal and non-verbal behavior. It involves paying attention to their body language, facial expressions, tone of voice, and choice of words. By being attuned to these signals, you can adjust your own communication style to match their preferences and create a deeper connection.

Building Trust: Trust is a crucial component of rapport. To build trust, it is important to demonstrate authenticity, empathy, and genuine interest in the other person. Show that you are actively listening and understanding their perspective. Avoid judgment or criticism and create a safe space for open and honest communication. Trust is the foundation upon which rapport can flourish.

Applying Rapport in Various Contexts

Rapport is a versatile skill that can be applied in various aspects of life and career. Whether you are in a business meeting, a personal relationship, or a coaching session, the ability to establish rapport can greatly enhance your effectiveness and influence.

In business and professional settings, rapport is essential for effective leadership, team collaboration, and client relationships. By building rapport with your team members, you create a positive and productive work environment. Rapport with clients allows you to understand their needs, build trust, and provide tailored solutions. Additionally, rapport is crucial in negotiations, as it helps to create a cooperative atmosphere and find mutually beneficial outcomes.

In personal relationships, rapport is the key to fostering intimacy, understanding, and connection. By establishing rapport with your partner, family members, or friends, you create a strong foundation for open and honest communication. Rapport allows you to empathize with others, understand their perspective, and resolve conflicts amicably.

In coaching and therapy, rapport is essential for creating a safe and supportive environment. By establishing rapport with your clients, you build trust and facilitate their personal growth and transformation. Rapport allows you to understand their needs, beliefs, and values, which in turn helps you tailor your coaching or therapy approach to their specific requirements.

Developing Rapport Skills

Building rapport is a skill that can be developed and refined with practice. Here are some strategies to enhance your rapport-building abilities:

Active Listening: Practice active listening by giving your full attention to the other person. Show genuine interest in what they are saying and respond with empathy and understanding. Avoid interrupting or imposing your own opinions. By actively listening, you demonstrate respect and create a space for open communication.

Empathy and Understanding: Cultivate empathy by putting yourself in the other person's shoes. Seek to understand their perspective, emotions, and needs. Show compassion and validate their experiences. By demonstrating empathy, you create a sense of connection and trust.

Flexibility and Adaptability: Be flexible in your communication style and adapt to the preferences of the other person. Pay attention to their body language, tone of voice, and choice of words. Adjust your own style accordingly to create a sense of familiarity and understanding.

Practice Non-Verbal Communication: Non-verbal cues play a significant role in building rapport. Pay attention to your own body language and ensure it aligns with your verbal communication.

Maintain eye contact, use open and relaxed gestures, and adopt a friendly and approachable posture.

Build Rapport with Yourself: Building rapport with others starts with building rapport with yourself. Cultivate self-awareness, self-acceptance, and self-confidence. When you are comfortable in your own skin, it becomes easier to establish rapport with others.

Remember, rapport is not about manipulation or control. It is about creating genuine connections and fostering positive relationships. By mastering the art of rapport, you can enhance your communication skills, build trust, and create meaningful connections in all areas of your life.

Active Listening

Active listening is a fundamental skill in effective communication and a key component of Neuro-Linguistic Programming (NLP). It involves fully engaging with the speaker, not only hearing their words but also understanding their message, emotions, and intentions. By actively listening, you can build rapport, gain valuable insights, and enhance your communication skills.

The Power of Active Listening

Active listening goes beyond simply hearing what someone is saying. It involves giving your full attention to the speaker, both verbally and non-verbally. When you actively listen, you demonstrate respect, empathy, and genuine interest in the other person. This creates a positive and supportive environment for effective communication.

By actively listening, you can:

Build Rapport: Active listening helps establish a strong connection with the speaker. When you show genuine interest in their thoughts and feelings, they feel valued and understood. This builds trust and rapport, which is essential for successful relationships, both personal and professional.

Understand the Speaker's Perspective: Active listening allows you to gain a deeper understanding of the speaker's thoughts, emotions, and intentions. By focusing on their words, tone, and body language, you can uncover valuable insights and perspectives that may not be explicitly stated. This understanding enables you to respond appropriately and effectively.

Enhance Communication: Active listening improves the

overall quality of communication. By fully engaging with the speaker, you can clarify any misunderstandings, ask relevant questions, and provide meaningful feedback. This promotes clear and effective communication, reducing the chances of miscommunication or conflicts.

Empower Others: When you actively listen, you empower the speaker to express themselves freely and openly. By creating a safe and non-judgmental space, you encourage them to share their thoughts, concerns, and ideas. This fosters a sense of empowerment and encourages collaboration and creativity.

Techniques for Active Listening

To become an active listener, you can employ various techniques and strategies. Here are some effective techniques to enhance your active listening skills:

Pay Attention: Give your full attention to the speaker. Eliminate distractions, such as electronic devices or internal thoughts, and focus on the speaker's words, tone, and body language. Maintain eye contact and use non-verbal cues, such as nodding or smiling, to show your engagement.

Avoid Interrupting: Allow the speaker to express themselves fully without interruption. Avoid jumping to conclusions or formulating responses before they have finished speaking. Instead, patiently listen and wait for appropriate pauses to ask clarifying questions or provide feedback.

Reflect and Paraphrase: Reflecting and paraphrasing the speaker's words demonstrates your understanding and validates their thoughts and feelings. Repeat or rephrase key points to ensure you have correctly interpreted their message. This also shows the speaker that you are actively engaged and interested in what they have to say.

Use Open-Ended Questions: Encourage the speaker to elaborate on their thoughts and feelings by asking open-ended questions. These questions cannot be answered with a simple "yes" or "no" and require the speaker to provide more detailed responses. This helps to deepen the conversation and gain a better understanding of their perspective.

Practice Empathy: Put yourself in the speaker's shoes and try to understand their emotions and experiences. Show empathy by acknowledging their feelings and validating their experiences. This creates a supportive and non-judgmental environment that encourages open and honest communication.

Be Mindful of Non-Verbal Cues: Pay attention to the speaker's body language, facial expressions, and tone of voice. These non-verbal cues can provide valuable insights into their emotions and intentions. By being aware of these cues, you can better understand the underlying message and respond appropriately.

Summarize and Recap: At the end of the conversation or during appropriate pauses, summarize and recap the main points discussed. This not only demonstrates your active listening skills but also ensures that both you and the speaker are on the same page. It helps to clarify any misunderstandings and provides an opportunity for further discussion if needed.

Benefits of Active Listening

Developing active listening skills can have numerous benefits in both personal and professional settings. Some of the key benefits include:

Improved Relationships: Active listening strengthens relationships by fostering trust, empathy, and understanding. It allows you to connect with others on a deeper level and build stronger bonds.

Enhanced Problem-Solving: By actively listening, you gain a better understanding of the challenges and concerns of others. This enables you to offer more effective solutions and support in problem-solving situations.

Increased Productivity: Active listening reduces misunderstandings and miscommunications, leading to increased productivity. Clear and effective communication ensures that tasks are completed accurately and efficiently.

Conflict Resolution: Active listening plays a crucial role in resolving conflicts. By understanding the perspectives of all parties involved, you can find common ground and work towards mutually beneficial solutions.

Personal Growth: Developing active listening skills can contribute to personal growth and self-awareness. It allows you to gain insights into your own communication patterns and areas for improvement.

Incorporating active listening into your daily interactions can have a profound impact on your relationships, communication skills, and overall success in life and career. By truly engaging with others and valuing their thoughts and feelings, you can unlock the power of active listening and harness its benefits.

Persuasive Language Patterns

Language is a powerful tool that can be used to influence and persuade others. In Neuro-Linguistic Programming (NLP), there are specific language patterns that can be employed to effectively communicate and persuade others. These persuasive language patterns can be used in various contexts, such as business negotiations, sales, and personal relationships, to achieve desired outcomes and build rapport with others.

The Power of Words

Words have the ability to shape our thoughts, emotions, and actions. By understanding and utilizing persuasive language patterns, you can enhance your communication skills and increase your ability to influence others. These language patterns are based on the principles of NLP and can help you establish rapport, build trust, and effectively convey your message.

1. Embedded Commands

Embedded commands are a powerful way to influence others without them even realizing it. By embedding a command within a sentence, you can subtly direct someone's thoughts or actions. For example, instead of saying, "You should consider buying this product," you can say, "As you consider buying this product, you'll realize its benefits." The embedded command "consider buying this product" is subtly communicated, increasing the likelihood of the person actually considering the purchase.

2. Presuppositions

Presuppositions are statements that assume the truth of something without explicitly stating it. By using presuppositions in your language, you can subtly influence someone's thinking. For example, instead of saying, "If you decide to join our team," you can say, "When you join our team, you'll experience the benefits of working with us." The presupposition that the person will join the team is subtly communicated, making it more likely for them to consider the opportunity.

3. Analogical Marking

Analogical marking involves using analogies or metaphors to convey your message. By comparing something unfamiliar to something familiar, you can help others understand and relate to your ideas. For example, instead of saying, "Our new software is user-friendly," you can say, "Our new software is as easy to use as riding a bike." The analogy of riding a bike helps the listener understand the concept of user-friendliness and creates a positive association with the software.

4. Sensory Language

Using sensory language can make your communication more vivid and engaging. By appealing to the senses, you can create a more immersive experience for the listener. For example, instead of saying, "This perfume smells good," you can say, "This perfume has a captivating scent that transports you to a field of blooming flowers." The sensory language of "captivating scent" and "field of blooming flowers" creates a more enticing description and enhances the listener's experience.

5. Future Pacing

Future pacing involves using language to create a vision of the future and influence someone's behavior or decision-making. By describing a positive outcome or result, you can motivate others to take action. For example, instead of saying, "You should start exercising," you can say, "Imagine how energized and fit you'll feel once you start exercising regularly." The future pacing of feeling energized and fit creates a compelling vision that can inspire the listener to take action.

6. Agreement Frames

Agreement frames are a way to guide someone towards agreement or compliance. By using language that assumes agreement, you can influence someone's perspective or decision. For example, instead of saying, "Do you agree with this proposal?" you can say, "How would you like to implement this proposal?" The agreement frame of "how would you like to implement" assumes agreement and encourages the listener to consider the proposal from a positive perspective.

7. Chunking

Chunking involves adjusting the level of detail in your communication to match the listener's preferences. By using language that is either more detailed or more general, you can effectively communicate with different individuals. For example, if you're speaking to someone who prefers a big-picture view, you can say, "In broad terms, our strategy is to increase market share." If you're speaking to someone who prefers more details, you can say, "Specifically, we plan to target new customer segments and launch targeted marketing campaigns." By adjusting your language to match the listener's preferences, you can enhance their understanding and engagement.

8. Meta Model

The Meta Model is a set of language patterns that can be used to challenge and clarify someone's thinking. By asking specific questions, you can help others expand their perspective and overcome limiting beliefs. For example, if someone says, "I can't achieve my goals," you can use the Meta Model to ask, "What specifically is preventing you from achieving your goals?" This question challenges the limiting belief and encourages the person to identify specific obstacles that can be addressed.

Persuasive language patterns are a valuable tool in NLP that can enhance your communication skills and increase your ability to influence others. By understanding and utilizing these patterns, you can effectively convey your message, build rapport, and achieve desired outcomes in various areas of your life. Whether you're negotiating a business deal, persuading someone to see your point of view, or building stronger relationships, mastering persuasive language patterns can significantly impact your success and fulfillment.

Non-Verbal Communication

Non-verbal communication plays a crucial role in our daily interactions, often conveying more information than words alone. In fact, research suggests that up to 93% of communication is non-verbal, making it a powerful tool for understanding others and expressing ourselves effectively. In this section, we will explore the importance of non-verbal communication and how it can be harnessed to enhance your personal and professional relationships.

The Power of Body Language

Body language refers to the non-verbal signals we send through our posture, gestures, facial expressions, and eye contact. These cues can reveal our true thoughts and emotions, often contradicting the words we speak. Understanding and interpreting body language can help you gain valuable insights into the thoughts and feelings of others, enabling you to respond appropriately and build rapport.

One key aspect of body language is posture. Standing or sitting upright with an open posture conveys confidence and approachability, while slouching or crossing your arms can signal defensiveness or disinterest. By consciously adjusting your posture, you can project a more positive and engaging presence, making others more receptive to your message.

Gestures also play a significant role in non-verbal communication. They can emphasize or reinforce verbal messages, convey emotions, or even substitute for words. For example, nodding your head while listening indicates understanding and agreement, while pointing can direct attention or indicate a specific object or direction. Being aware of your own gestures and observing those of others can help you better understand their intentions and respond accordingly.

Facial expressions are another essential component of non-verbal communication. Our faces are incredibly expressive, capable of conveying a wide range of emotions. A smile, for instance, can indicate friendliness and warmth, while a furrowed brow may signal confusion or concern. By paying attention to facial expressions, you can gauge the emotional state of others and adjust your communication style accordingly.

Eye contact is a powerful non-verbal cue that can establish trust and connection. Maintaining appropriate eye contact shows attentiveness and interest in the conversation, while avoiding eye contact can be perceived as disengagement or dishonesty. However, it is important to note that cultural norms and individual preferences may influence the appropriate level of eye contact, so it is essential to be mindful of these factors in different contexts.

Enhancing Communication through Non-Verbal Cues

In addition to understanding and interpreting non-verbal cues, you can also utilize them to enhance your own communication skills. By consciously aligning your non-verbal signals with your verbal message, you can create a more impactful and persuasive communication style.

First and foremost, it is crucial to be aware of your own body language. Pay attention to your posture, gestures, and facial expressions, ensuring they align with the message you want to convey. For example, if you are delivering a presentation on a topic you are passionate about, your body language should reflect enthusiasm and confidence. By consciously adjusting your non-verbal cues, you can enhance your credibility and engage your audience more effectively.

Mirroring is another powerful technique that can foster rapport and connection. Mirroring involves subtly imitating the body language of the person you are interacting with, such as matching their posture, gestures, or even their speech patterns. This technique can create a sense of familiarity and trust, making the other person more receptive to your message. However, it is important to use mirroring subtly and respectfully, as excessive imitation can come across as insincere or manipulative.

Non-verbal cues can also be used to regulate and manage the flow of conversation. For instance, leaning forward slightly can signal interest and encourage the other person to continue speaking, while leaning back may indicate a desire to conclude the conversation. By utilizing these cues strategically, you can guide the interaction and ensure effective communication.

Non-Verbal Communication in Professional Settings

In professional settings, non-verbal communication plays a crucial role in establishing credibility, building relationships, and conveying leadership. By mastering the art of non-verbal communication, you can enhance your professional presence and increase your chances of success.

When attending job interviews or important meetings, paying attention to your non-verbal cues can make a significant difference. Projecting confidence through your posture, maintaining appropriate eye contact, and using gestures to emphasize key points can help you make a positive impression and convey your competence and professionalism.

In team settings, non-verbal cues can also be used to foster collaboration and build rapport. Active listening, demonstrated through nodding, maintaining eye contact, and using appropriate facial expressions, shows respect and engagement. By being mindful of your non-verbal signals, you can create an inclusive and supportive environment that encourages open communication and collaboration.

Non-verbal communication is also essential in leadership roles. Leaders who can effectively utilize non-verbal cues can inspire and motivate their teams, convey authority and confidence, and build trust. By aligning their non-verbal signals with their verbal messages, leaders can create a compelling and influential presence that inspires others to follow their lead.

Non-verbal communication is a powerful tool that can greatly enhance your personal and professional relationships. By understanding and utilizing non-verbal cues effectively, you can improve your communication skills, build rapport, and convey your message with greater impact. Whether in personal interactions or professional settings, mastering the art of non-verbal communication can unlock new levels of success and fulfillment in your life and career.

CHAPTER 5
LEADERSHIP AND INFLUENCE

Leadership is a crucial skill in both personal and professional life. Whether you are leading a team at work, managing a project, or simply striving to become a better version of yourself, the ability to influence others is essential. Neuro-Linguistic Programming (NLP) offers powerful techniques and strategies that can help you unlock your leadership potential and become a more effective influencer.

At its core, leadership is about inspiring and motivating others to achieve a common goal. NLP provides a framework for understanding human behavior and communication patterns, allowing you to tap into the subconscious mind of others and influence their thoughts, emotions, and actions. By mastering the principles of NLP, you can become a more persuasive and influential leader.

One of the key concepts in NLP is the understanding that people have different communication styles and preferences. Some individuals are more visually oriented, while others are more auditory or kinesthetic. As a leader, it is important to adapt your communication style to match the preferences of your team members. By doing so, you can establish rapport and build trust, which are essential for effective leadership.

NLP offers a range of techniques that can help you establish rapport with others. One such technique is mirroring and matching, where you subtly mimic the body language, speech patterns, and even breathing of the person you are communicating with. This technique helps create a sense of familiarity and connection, making it easier to influence and persuade others.

Another powerful NLP technique for leadership and influence is the use of language patterns. Our choice of words can have a profound impact on how others perceive and respond to us. By using persuasive language patterns, such as embedded commands and presuppositions, you can subtly influence the thoughts and actions of others. For example, instead of saying "You should do this," you can say "Imagine how much better things would be if you did this." This subtle shift in language can make a significant difference in how your message is received.

In addition to language patterns, NLP also emphasizes the importance of non-verbal communication. Research has shown that a significant portion of our communication is conveyed through body language, facial expressions, and tone of voice. As a leader, it is important to be aware of your own non-verbal cues and to interpret the non-verbal cues of others. By aligning your non-verbal communication with your verbal message, you can enhance your influence and credibility.

Another aspect of leadership and influence that NLP addresses is the ability to manage and resolve conflicts. Conflict is inevitable in any group or organization, and effective leaders are skilled at navigating and resolving conflicts in a constructive manner. NLP provides techniques for reframing conflicts, understanding different perspectives, and finding win-win solutions. By applying these techniques, you can create a harmonious and productive work environment.

Furthermore, NLP can help you develop your emotional intelligence, which is a critical skill for effective leadership. Emotional intelligence involves the ability to recognize and manage your own emotions, as well as the emotions of others. By understanding the underlying emotions and motivations of your team members, you can better connect with them and inspire them to perform at their best.

Lastly, NLP can assist you in developing your personal leadership style. By modeling the behaviors and strategies of successful leaders, you can learn to embody their qualities and achieve similar results. NLP offers techniques for modeling excellence, allowing you to identify the specific skills, beliefs, and behaviors that contribute to leadership success. By adopting these qualities and integrating them into your own leadership style, you can become a more influential and impactful leader.

In conclusion, leadership and influence are essential skills for success in both personal and professional life. Neuro-Linguistic Programming (NLP) provides a powerful toolkit for enhancing your leadership abilities and becoming a more effective influencer. By understanding and applying the principles of NLP, you can establish rapport, communicate persuasively, manage conflicts, and inspire others to achieve their full potential. Whether you are leading a team, managing a project, or striving for personal growth, NLP can unlock your leadership potential and propel you towards success.

Effective Decision Making

Making decisions is an integral part of our daily lives. From the moment we wake up in the morning to the time we go to bed at night, we are constantly faced with choices that shape our experiences and determine our outcomes. Whether it's deciding what to wear, what to eat for breakfast, or which route to take to work, our ability to make effective decisions can greatly impact our success in life and career.

Neuro-Linguistic Programming (NLP) offers powerful techniques and strategies that can enhance our decision-making skills and help us make choices that align with our goals and values. By understanding the underlying processes of decision making and utilizing NLP techniques, we can unlock our potential and make decisions that lead to success and fulfillment.

The Decision-Making Process

Before delving into the specific NLP techniques for effective decision making, it's important to understand the decision-making process itself. Decision making involves several stages, including gathering information, evaluating options, weighing pros and cons, and ultimately making a choice. However, many individuals struggle with decision making due to various factors such as fear of making the wrong choice, analysis paralysis, or lack of clarity about their goals.

NLP provides a framework for improving decision making by addressing these challenges and enhancing our cognitive processes. By utilizing NLP techniques, we can gain clarity, overcome limiting beliefs, and tap into our unconscious mind to make decisions that align with our values and aspirations.

Anchoring for Clarity and Confidence

One powerful NLP technique that can enhance decision making is anchoring. Anchoring involves associating a specific state of mind or emotion with a physical or mental trigger. By anchoring positive states such as clarity and confidence to a specific gesture or word, we can access these states whenever we need to make a decision.

To utilize anchoring for effective decision making, start by recalling a time when you felt confident and clear-headed. Remember the details of that experience, including the sights, sounds, and feelings associated with it. As you vividly recall this experience, create an anchor by performing a specific gesture or saying a word that represents that state of confidence and clarity.

Practice anchoring by repeating this process several times, reinforcing the association between the anchor and the desired state. Then, when faced with a decision, activate the anchor by performing the gesture or saying the word. This will help you access the confident and clear-headed state, enabling you to make decisions with greater certainty and conviction.

Reframing Limiting Beliefs

Another crucial aspect of effective decision making is addressing and reframing limiting beliefs. Limiting beliefs are deeply ingrained thoughts or beliefs that hold us back from reaching our full potential. They often stem from past experiences or societal conditioning and can greatly influence our decision-making process.

NLP offers powerful techniques for identifying and reframing limiting beliefs. Start by becoming aware of any negative or self-limiting thoughts that arise when making decisions. Ask yourself if these thoughts are based on facts or if they are simply assumptions or interpretations.

Once you have identified a limiting belief, challenge it by asking yourself if it is serving you or holding you back. Replace the limiting belief with a more empowering belief that aligns with your goals and values. For example, if you have a belief that you are not capable of starting your own business, reframe it to "I have the skills and resources to start and succeed in my own business."

By reframing limiting beliefs, you can shift your mindset and approach decision making with a more positive and empowered perspective. This will enable you to make decisions that align with your true potential and aspirations.

Utilizing Visualization and Mental Rehearsal

Visualization and mental rehearsal are powerful NLP techniques that can greatly enhance decision making. By vividly imagining the outcomes of different choices and mentally rehearsing the decision-making process, you can gain clarity and confidence in your decision-making abilities.

Start by visualizing the potential outcomes of each decision you are considering. Imagine yourself in each scenario, experiencing the emotions, sensations, and consequences associated with each choice. Pay attention to how each outcome aligns with your goals and values.

Next, mentally rehearse the decision-making process itself. Imagine yourself gathering information, evaluating options, and weighing the pros and cons. Visualize yourself making the decision with confidence and conviction, knowing that it aligns with your goals and values.

By utilizing visualization and mental rehearsal, you can tap into the power of your unconscious mind and gain valuable insights and clarity. This will enable you to make decisions with greater confidence and certainty, knowing that you have thoroughly considered the potential outcomes.

Trusting Your Intuition

In addition to utilizing NLP techniques, it's important to trust your intuition when making decisions. Intuition is a powerful tool that can provide valuable insights and guidance, often beyond what our conscious mind can comprehend.

To tap into your intuition, practice quieting your mind through meditation or mindfulness techniques. Create space for your intuition to emerge by letting go of excessive analysis and allowing yourself to connect with your inner wisdom.

When faced with a decision, take a moment to tune into your intuition. Pay attention to any gut feelings, hunches, or subtle nudges that arise. Trust that your intuition is guiding you towards the best choice for your highest good.

By combining NLP techniques with trusting your intuition, you can make decisions that are aligned with your goals, values, and inner wisdom. This holistic approach to decision making will empower

53

you to navigate life and career with confidence and clarity.

In conclusion, effective decision making is a crucial skill for success in life and career. By harnessing the power of NLP techniques such as anchoring, reframing limiting beliefs, utilizing visualization and mental rehearsal, and trusting your intuition, you can enhance your decision-making abilities and make choices that align with your goals and values. Embrace the power of NLP and unlock your potential for making effective decisions that lead to success and fulfillment.

Negotiation and Conflict Resolution

Negotiation and conflict resolution are essential skills in both personal and professional life. Whether you are dealing with a disagreement with a colleague, a difficult client, or a challenging personal relationship, the ability to effectively negotiate and resolve conflicts can make a significant difference in achieving positive outcomes. In this section, we will explore how Neuro-Linguistic Programming (NLP) can be applied to enhance your negotiation skills and facilitate successful conflict resolution.

Understanding the Dynamics of Negotiation

Negotiation is a process of communication and compromise between two or more parties with conflicting interests. It requires a delicate balance of assertiveness, empathy, and problem-solving skills. NLP provides valuable tools and techniques to understand and influence the underlying dynamics of negotiation.

One of the fundamental principles of NLP is the understanding that people have different communication and thinking styles. By recognizing and adapting to these styles, you can establish rapport and build trust, which are crucial elements in successful negotiation. NLP teaches you to observe and interpret verbal and non-verbal cues, allowing you to better understand the needs, desires, and motivations of the other party.

Building Rapport for Effective Negotiation

Building rapport is a key component of successful negotiation. When people feel a connection and trust with each other, they are more likely to engage in open and constructive dialogue. NLP offers various techniques to establish rapport quickly and effectively.

One such technique is mirroring and matching. Mirroring

involves subtly imitating the other person's body language, gestures, and speech patterns. Matching involves adopting a similar communication style, such as using similar words or phrases. These techniques help create a sense of familiarity and similarity, fostering a positive atmosphere for negotiation.

Another powerful NLP technique for building rapport is pacing and leading. Pacing involves aligning yourself with the other person's perspective and acknowledging their point of view. By demonstrating understanding and empathy, you can establish a foundation of trust. Once rapport is established, leading allows you to gently guide the negotiation towards a mutually beneficial outcome.

Effective Communication in Negotiation

Effective communication is crucial in negotiation. NLP provides valuable insights and techniques to enhance your communication skills and ensure your message is understood and received positively.

One important aspect of effective communication is active listening. NLP teaches you to listen attentively, not only to the words being spoken but also to the underlying emotions and intentions. By actively listening, you can gain a deeper understanding of the other person's needs and concerns, allowing you to address them effectively during the negotiation process.

NLP also emphasizes the use of persuasive language patterns. These patterns involve using specific words and phrases that influence and persuade others. By employing language patterns such as embedded commands, presuppositions, and sensory language, you can subtly guide the negotiation in your desired direction.

Resolving Conflicts with NLP

Conflict resolution is an essential skill in both personal and professional relationships. NLP offers effective strategies and techniques to resolve conflicts and reach mutually satisfactory solutions.

One powerful NLP technique for conflict resolution is reframing. Reframing involves changing the way you perceive and interpret a situation. By reframing conflicts as opportunities for growth and understanding, you can shift the focus from blame and negativity to collaboration and problem-solving.

Another valuable NLP technique for conflict resolution is the use of perceptual positions. Perceptual positions involve adopting different perspectives to gain a broader understanding of the conflict. By stepping into the shoes of the other person and viewing the situation from their point of view, you can develop empathy and find common ground for resolution.

NLP also emphasizes the importance of maintaining a positive mindset during conflict resolution. By focusing on solutions rather than dwelling on problems, you can create an environment conducive to finding mutually beneficial outcomes.

Applying NLP in Negotiation and Conflict Resolution

To apply NLP effectively in negotiation and conflict resolution, it is essential to practice and integrate the techniques into your communication style. Here are some practical steps to apply NLP principles in these situations:

Establish rapport: Use mirroring and matching techniques to build rapport quickly. Pay attention to the other person's body language, tone of voice, and choice of words.

Active listening: Practice active listening by giving your full attention to the other person. Listen not only to their words but also to their emotions and intentions.

Use persuasive language patterns: Incorporate persuasive language patterns such as embedded commands, presuppositions, and sensory language to influence and guide the negotiation process.

Reframe conflicts: Shift your perspective on conflicts by reframing them as opportunities for growth and understanding. Focus on finding solutions rather than dwelling on problems.

Adopt perceptual positions: Step into the shoes of the other person and view the conflict from their perspective. Develop empathy and seek common ground for resolution.

Maintain a positive mindset: Stay focused on positive outcomes and maintain a constructive attitude throughout the negotiation and conflict resolution process.

By integrating these NLP techniques into your negotiation and conflict resolution skills, you can enhance your ability to reach mutually beneficial agreements and resolve conflicts effectively. NLP provides a powerful framework for understanding and influencing human behavior, enabling you to navigate challenging situations with confidence and success.

Presentation Skills

Presenting information effectively is a crucial skill in both personal and professional settings. Whether you are delivering a presentation to a large audience, pitching an idea to your colleagues, or simply sharing your thoughts in a meeting, the way you present can greatly impact how your message is received. In this section, we will explore how Neuro-Linguistic Programming (NLP) can enhance your presentation skills and help you become a more confident and persuasive communicator.

The Power of Rapport in Presentations

Rapport is the foundation of effective communication, and it plays a significant role in presentations as well. When you establish rapport with your audience, you create a connection that allows them to trust and engage with you. NLP offers various techniques to build rapport effortlessly.

One powerful technique is mirroring and matching. By subtly mirroring the body language, gestures, and even the tone of voice of your audience, you can establish a sense of familiarity and connection. This technique helps to create a harmonious atmosphere and makes your audience more receptive to your message.

Another technique is pacing and leading. Pacing involves aligning yourself with your audience's current state of mind or understanding. By acknowledging their perspective and using language that resonates with them, you can build rapport and establish credibility. Once rapport is established, you can then lead your audience towards your desired outcome by introducing new ideas or perspectives.

Utilizing Persuasive Language Patterns

Language is a powerful tool in presentations, and NLP provides a range of persuasive language patterns that can help you influence and engage your audience. One such pattern is the use of embedded commands. By embedding commands within your speech, you can subtly guide your audience's thoughts and actions. For example, instead of saying, "You should consider this option," you can say, "As you consider this option, you may find it beneficial."

Another effective language pattern is the use of presuppositions. Presuppositions are statements that assume the truth of something without explicitly stating it. By using presuppositions, you can subtly influence your audience's thinking and create a sense of inevitability. For example, instead of saying, "If you implement this strategy, you will see positive results," you can say, "When you implement this strategy, you will notice the positive results."

Engaging Non-Verbal Communication

Non-verbal communication plays a significant role in presentations, often conveying more than words alone. NLP offers techniques to enhance your non-verbal communication and make your presentations more engaging and impactful.

One important aspect of non-verbal communication is body language. By being aware of your own body language and making conscious adjustments, you can convey confidence, openness, and enthusiasm. Maintaining good posture, making eye contact, and using appropriate gestures can help you establish a strong presence and connect with your audience on a deeper level.

Another aspect of non-verbal communication is voice modulation. Your tone, pitch, and pace of speech can greatly influence how your message is received. NLP techniques can help you develop a more dynamic and engaging speaking style. By varying your voice to emphasize key points, using pauses for effect, and adjusting your pace to match the content, you can captivate your audience and keep them engaged throughout your presentation.

Creating Compelling Visuals

Visual aids are an essential component of many presentations, and NLP can help you create visuals that are both visually appealing and impactful. When designing your slides or visual aids, consider the following NLP principles:

Use clear and concise language: Keep your text minimal and use bullet points or keywords to convey your message. Avoid cluttering your slides with excessive information that can overwhelm your audience.

Utilize visual metaphors: Visual metaphors can help simplify complex concepts and make them more relatable. Use images or symbols that represent your ideas and reinforce your message.

Incorporate colors strategically: Colors can evoke emotions and influence how your audience perceives your message. Choose colors that align with the tone and content of your presentation. For example, warm colors like red and orange can convey energy and excitement, while cool colors like blue and green can create a sense of calm and trust.

Use visuals to tell a story: Instead of relying solely on text, use visuals to tell a story and engage your audience on an emotional level. Incorporate images, graphs, or charts that support your narrative and help your audience visualize your ideas.

Overcoming Presentation Anxiety

Many people experience anxiety when it comes to public speaking and presentations. NLP techniques can help you overcome presentation anxiety and perform at your best.

One effective technique is anchoring. Anchoring involves associating a specific state of mind or emotion with a physical gesture or trigger. By creating a positive anchor, such as pressing your thumb and forefinger together, you can access a state of confidence and calmness whenever you need it. Practice anchoring before your presentation, and use the anchor during your presentation to help you stay focused and composed.

Visualization and mental rehearsal are also powerful tools for overcoming anxiety. Before your presentation, take some time to visualize yourself delivering a successful and engaging presentation. Imagine yourself speaking confidently, connecting with your audience, and receiving positive feedback. This mental rehearsal can help reduce anxiety and build your confidence.

NLP offers valuable techniques to enhance your presentation skills and become a more confident and persuasive communicator. By building rapport, utilizing persuasive language patterns, enhancing non-verbal communication, creating compelling visuals, and overcoming presentation anxiety, you can deliver impactful presentations that captivate your audience and achieve your desired outcomes.

THE MINDTECH
INSTITUTE

Now, you can become a fully qualified Hypnotherapist, NLP Master Practitioner, Master Life Coach, Counsellor and more by simply studying online. More accredited Diplomas (Associate Degrees) and other courses are also available at www.themindtechinstitute.com

www.mti.edu.au

CHAPTER SIX
HEALTH AND WELLNESS

Mind-Body Connection

The mind and body are intricately connected, and understanding this connection is crucial for unlocking your potential and achieving success in all areas of your life. Neuro-Linguistic Programming (NLP) provides powerful tools and techniques to harness this mind-body connection and create positive change.

The Power of the Mind-Body Connection

The mind and body are not separate entities but rather two aspects of the same whole. They constantly influence and interact with each other, shaping our thoughts, emotions, behaviors, and physical well-being. The mind-body connection is a fundamental principle in NLP, as it recognizes that our thoughts and beliefs have a direct impact on our physical health and vice versa.

Research has shown that our thoughts and emotions can affect our immune system, cardiovascular health, digestion, and overall well-being. Negative thoughts and stress can weaken the immune system, increase blood pressure, and contribute to the development of chronic diseases. On the other hand, positive thoughts, relaxation, and mindfulness can enhance our physical health and promote healing.

Using NLP to Enhance the Mind-Body Connection

NLP offers a range of techniques to enhance the mind-body

connection and promote holistic well-being. By understanding and utilizing these techniques, you can improve your physical health, manage stress, and cultivate a positive mindset.

1. Anchoring: Anchoring is a powerful NLP technique that allows you to associate a specific state of mind or emotion with a physical anchor. By creating an anchor, such as a touch or a word, you can access a desired state whenever you need it. For example, if you want to feel confident before a presentation, you can anchor that feeling by pressing your thumb and index finger together. Whenever you need to access that confidence, you can simply press your thumb and index finger together to trigger the anchored state.

2. Visualization and Mental Rehearsal: Visualization is a technique used in NLP to create vivid mental images of desired outcomes. By visualizing yourself achieving your goals or engaging in positive behaviors, you can program your mind to work towards those outcomes. Mental rehearsal takes visualization a step further by mentally practicing specific actions or scenarios. This technique can be used to improve performance in sports, public speaking, or any other area where practice is essential.

3. Managing Emotions: NLP provides techniques for managing and transforming negative emotions. By understanding the underlying patterns and beliefs that contribute to negative emotions, you can reframe them and create more empowering emotional states. For example, if you tend to feel anxious in social situations, NLP techniques can help you reframe your beliefs about social interactions and replace anxiety with confidence.

4. Stress Management: Stress is a common problem in today's fast-paced world, and it can have a detrimental impact on both our physical and mental health. NLP offers effective strategies for managing stress and promoting relaxation. Techniques such as deep breathing, progressive muscle relaxation, and guided imagery can help you reduce stress levels and restore balance to your mind and body.

5. Creating a Positive Mindset: A positive mindset is essential for success in all areas of life. NLP can help you cultivate a positive mindset by identifying and reframing limiting beliefs, developing empowering self-talk, and focusing on solutions rather than problems. By adopting a positive mindset, you can overcome obstacles, maintain motivation, and attract success into your life.

Integrating Mind-Body Connection into Daily Life

To fully harness the power of the mind-body connection, it is important to integrate these principles and techniques into your daily life. Here are some practical steps you can take:

Practice mindfulness: Engage in activities that promote present-moment awareness, such as meditation, yoga, or tai chi. These practices can help you develop a deeper connection with your body and cultivate a sense of inner calm.

Pay attention to your thoughts: Become aware of your thoughts and the impact they have on your emotions and physical sensations. Whenever you notice negative or limiting thoughts, challenge them and replace them with more positive and empowering ones.

Take care of your physical health: Engage in regular exercise, eat a balanced diet, and get enough sleep. Physical well-being is closely linked to mental and emotional well-being, so taking care of your body is essential for overall success and happiness.

Use NLP techniques consistently: Incorporate anchoring, visualization, and other NLP techniques into your daily routine. Practice them regularly to reinforce positive patterns and create lasting change.

By embracing the mind-body connection and utilizing NLP techniques, you can unlock your potential, achieve success, and experience greater well-being in all areas of your life. Remember, your mind and body are powerful allies on your journey towards personal and professional growth.

Overcoming Bad Habits

In our journey towards personal and professional success, we often find ourselves hindered by bad habits that hold us back from reaching our full potential. These habits can manifest in various aspects of our lives, from health and wellness to relationships and career. However, with the power of Neuro-Linguistic Programming (NLP), we can effectively overcome these detrimental patterns and replace them with positive behaviors that propel us towards success.

Understanding the Nature of Bad Habits

Before we delve into the techniques and strategies for overcoming bad habits, it is essential to understand their nature and how they are formed. Habits, whether good or bad, are deeply ingrained patterns of behavior that we perform automatically and unconsciously. They are often triggered by specific cues or situations and provide us with a sense of comfort or familiarity.

Bad habits can range from minor annoyances to major obstacles in our lives. They can include behaviors such as procrastination, excessive worrying, overeating, smoking, or negative self-talk. These habits not only hinder our progress but also impact our overall well-being and happiness.

The Power of NLP in Overcoming Bad Habits

Neuro-Linguistic Programming offers a powerful set of tools and techniques that can help us break free from the grip of bad habits. By understanding the underlying processes of habit formation and utilizing NLP strategies, we can reprogram our minds and create new, positive patterns of behavior.

NLP techniques such as reframing, anchoring, and visualization can be particularly effective in overcoming bad habits. Reframing involves changing the way we perceive and interpret situations, allowing us to view them from a more empowering perspective. Anchoring helps us associate new behaviors with positive emotions, creating a strong motivation to break free from old habits. Visualization allows us to mentally rehearse new behaviors and outcomes, reinforcing our commitment to change.

Identifying and Analyzing Bad Habits

The first step in overcoming bad habits is to identify and analyze them. Take some time to reflect on the habits that are holding you back and causing you distress. Consider the triggers or situations that lead to these habits and the negative consequences they have on your life.

Once you have identified your bad habits, it is essential to analyze the underlying beliefs and emotions associated with them. Often, our habits are rooted in deep-seated beliefs or unresolved emotions. By uncovering these underlying factors, you can gain valuable insights into the reasons behind your habits and begin the process of transformation.

Creating a Plan for Change

Once you have identified and analyzed your bad habits, it is time to create a plan for change. Start by setting clear and specific goals for overcoming each habit. Make sure your goals are realistic and achievable, and break them down into smaller, manageable steps.

Next, utilize NLP techniques to reframe your mindset and beliefs around the habit. Challenge any negative self-talk or limiting beliefs that may be reinforcing the habit. Replace them with positive affirmations and empowering beliefs that support your desired change.

Utilizing NLP Techniques for Overcoming Bad Habits

NLP offers a range of techniques that can be applied to overcome bad habits effectively. Here are a few techniques you can incorporate into your journey towards change:

Anchoring: Create a physical or mental anchor that you can use to interrupt the habit loop and replace it with a more positive behavior. For example, if you are trying to quit smoking, you can create an anchor by snapping your fingers every time you feel the urge to smoke and then immediately engaging in a healthier activity.

Reframing: Change the way you perceive the habit by reframing it in a more positive light. For example, if you have a habit of procrastinating, reframe it as an opportunity to prioritize and focus on what truly matters.

Visualization: Use the power of visualization to mentally rehearse the new behavior you want to adopt. Imagine yourself engaging in the desired behavior and experiencing the positive outcomes that come with it. This visualization will help reinforce your commitment to change.

Pattern Interrupt: Interrupt the habit loop by introducing a new, positive behavior whenever you feel the urge to engage in the bad habit. For example, if you have a habit of stress eating, you can interrupt the pattern by going for a walk or practicing deep breathing instead.

Submodalities: Explore the sensory components of your habit and identify any submodalities that intensify the habit loop. For example, if you have a habit of biting your nails, pay attention to the sensations and images associated with the habit. By changing these submodalities, you can weaken the habit's hold on you.

Cultivating Patience and Persistence

Overcoming bad habits is not an overnight process. It requires patience, persistence, and a commitment to personal growth. There may be setbacks along the way, but it is crucial to view them as learning opportunities rather than failures. Be kind to yourself and celebrate even the smallest victories.

Remember, breaking free from bad habits is a journey of self-discovery and transformation. By harnessing the power of NLP and implementing the techniques outlined in this section, you can overcome your bad habits and unlock your true potential for success in all areas of your life.

Stress Management

Stress is an inevitable part of life. Whether it's due to work pressures, personal challenges, or unexpected events, stress can have a significant impact on our overall well-being and success. However, with the power of Neuro-Linguistic Programming (NLP), you can learn effective strategies to manage and reduce stress, allowing you to lead a more balanced and fulfilling life.

Understanding Stress

Before we delve into the techniques and strategies for managing stress, it's important to understand what stress is and how it affects us. Stress is the body's natural response to perceived threats or challenges. When we encounter a stressful situation, our body releases stress hormones, such as cortisol and adrenaline, which trigger the "fight or flight" response.

While stress can be beneficial in certain situations, chronic or excessive stress can have detrimental effects on our physical and mental health. It can lead to a range of symptoms, including fatigue, irritability, difficulty concentrating, sleep disturbances, and even more serious conditions like anxiety and depression.

The NLP Approach to Stress Management

Neuro-Linguistic Programming offers a unique and effective approach to managing stress. By understanding the underlying patterns of our thoughts, emotions, and behaviors, we can gain control over our stress response and develop healthier coping mechanisms. Here are some powerful NLP techniques that can help you effectively manage stress:

1. Reframing: One of the fundamental principles of NLP is reframing, which involves changing the way we perceive and interpret stressful situations. By reframing our thoughts and beliefs, we can shift our perspective and find more empowering meanings in challenging circumstances. For example, instead of viewing a demanding work project as overwhelming, we can reframe it as an opportunity for growth and development.

2. Anchoring: Anchoring is a powerful NLP technique that allows us to access positive emotional states at will. By associating a specific physical or mental cue with a positive state, such as relaxation or calmness, we can anchor that state and use it to counteract stress. For instance, you can create an anchor by pressing your thumb and forefinger together while feeling deeply relaxed. By practicing this anchor regularly, you can quickly access a state of relaxation whenever you feel stressed.

3. Regression Therapy: Regression Therapy which is part of the hypnosis training that is available at The MindTech Institute online and in class, is a specialized hypnosis technique that focuses on releasing negative emotions and limiting beliefs associated with past events. By revisiting and reframing past experiences, you can let go of emotional baggage and reduce the impact of past stressors on your present life. Regression Therapy can be a powerful tool for managing stress, as it allows you to create a more positive and empowering outlook on life.

4. Mindfulness and Meditation: Mindfulness and meditation practices are integral to stress management in NLP. By cultivating present-moment awareness and practicing mindfulness, you can reduce stress and increase your ability to respond to challenges in a calm and centered manner. Regular meditation can also help you develop a greater sense of self-awareness, allowing you to recognize and manage stress triggers more effectively.

5. Language Patterns: The language we use has a profound impact on our stress levels. NLP teaches us to use positive and empowering language patterns to reframe stressful situations and reduce their impact on our well-being. By consciously choosing our words and focusing on solutions rather than problems, we can shift our mindset and create a more positive and stress-free environment.

6. Self-Care and Relaxation Techniques: In addition to the NLP techniques mentioned above, it's essential to incorporate self-care and relaxation techniques into your daily routine. Engaging in activities that bring you joy and relaxation, such as exercise, hobbies, spending time in nature, or practicing deep breathing exercises, can significantly reduce stress levels and promote overall well-being.

Implementing NLP for Stress Management

To effectively manage stress using NLP, it's important to integrate these techniques into your daily life. Consistency and practice are key to reaping the benefits of NLP for stress management. Here are some steps you can take to implement NLP strategies into your routine:

Start by identifying your stress triggers and patterns. Pay attention to the situations, thoughts, and emotions that tend to cause stress in your life.

Practice reframing stressful situations by consciously choosing more empowering interpretations and meanings.

Create anchors for positive emotional states, such as relaxation or calmness, and practice using them whenever you feel stressed.

Explore Regression Therapy techniques to release negative emotions and limiting beliefs associated with past stressors.

Incorporate mindfulness and meditation practices into your daily routine to cultivate present-moment awareness and reduce stress.

Pay attention to the language you use and consciously choose positive and empowering language patterns to reframe stressful situations.

Prioritize self-care and relaxation techniques, making time for activities that bring you joy and relaxation on a regular basis.

By implementing these NLP techniques and strategies, you can effectively manage and reduce stress in your life. Remember, stress management is a lifelong journey, and it requires consistent effort and practice. With the power of NLP, you have the tools to transform your relationship with stress and create a more balanced and fulfilling life.

Creating a Positive Mindset

A positive mindset is a powerful tool that can greatly impact your life and career. It is the foundation upon which success is built. When you have a positive mindset, you approach challenges with optimism, believe in your abilities, and maintain a resilient attitude in the face of adversity. In this section, we will explore how Neuro-Linguistic Programming (NLP) can help you create and maintain a positive mindset.

The Power of Positive Thinking

Positive thinking is not just a cliché; it is a scientifically proven concept that has a profound impact on our mental and physical well-being. When you think positively, you activate the reward centers in your brain, releasing feel-good chemicals such as dopamine and serotonin. This not only improves your mood but also enhances your cognitive abilities, creativity, and problem-solving skills.

NLP provides powerful techniques to help you cultivate a positive mindset. One such technique is reframing, which involves changing the way you perceive a situation. By reframing negative thoughts or experiences into positive ones, you can shift your perspective and find opportunities for growth and learning.

The Language of Positivity

The language we use has a significant impact on our mindset. By consciously choosing positive and empowering words, we can reprogram our subconscious mind to focus on solutions rather than problems. NLP teaches us to use language patterns that promote positivity and success.

Affirmations are a powerful tool in NLP for creating a positive mindset. By repeating positive statements about yourself and your goals, you can rewire your brain to believe in your abilities and attract success. For example, instead of saying, "I can't do it," you can reframe it as, "I am capable of overcoming any challenge."

Anchoring Positive States

Anchoring is a technique in NLP that allows you to associate a specific physical or mental state with a desired emotion or mindset. By creating an anchor, such as a touch or a word, you can trigger a positive state whenever you need it. This can be particularly useful in high-pressure situations or when you need a boost of confidence.

To create an anchor for a positive mindset, think of a time when you felt confident, motivated, or happy. Recall the details of that experience, including the sights, sounds, and feelings associated with it. Then, choose a physical gesture or word that you can use as an anchor. Practice associating that gesture or word with the positive state until it becomes automatic.

Visualization and Mental Rehearsal

Visualization is a powerful technique used in NLP to create a positive mindset. By vividly imagining yourself achieving your goals and experiencing success, you activate the same neural pathways in your brain as if you were actually doing it. This helps to build confidence, motivation, and belief in your abilities.

Mental rehearsal is a technique closely related to visualization. It involves mentally rehearsing a specific task or situation, imagining yourself performing it successfully. By repeatedly rehearsing in your mind, you build neural pathways that support the actual performance of the task. This not only enhances your skills but also boosts your confidence and reduces anxiety.

Gratitude and Appreciation

Practicing gratitude and appreciation is a simple yet powerful way to cultivate a positive mindset. By focusing on the things you are grateful for, you shift your attention away from negativity and scarcity. This helps to rewire your brain to notice and appreciate the abundance and opportunities around you.

NLP offers techniques to enhance the practice of gratitude and appreciation. One such technique is the "Three Good Things" exercise. At the end of each day, write down three things that went well or that you are grateful for. This exercise helps to reframe your mindset and train your brain to focus on the positive aspects of your life.

Overcoming Limiting Beliefs

Limiting beliefs are negative thoughts or beliefs that hold us back from reaching our full potential. They often stem from past experiences or societal conditioning. NLP provides powerful techniques to identify and overcome limiting beliefs, allowing you to create a positive mindset.

One technique is called "belief change." This involves challenging and reframing the negative beliefs that are holding you back. By questioning the validity of these beliefs and replacing them with positive and empowering ones, you can transform your mindset and open yourself up to new possibilities.

Surrounding Yourself with Positivity

The people and environment we surround ourselves with have a significant impact on our mindset. To create and maintain a positive mindset, it is important to surround yourself with positive and supportive individuals who uplift and inspire you.

NLP teaches us to model excellence by studying and emulating the behaviors and mindset of successful individuals. By surrounding yourself with positive role models, you can learn from their experiences and adopt their positive mindset.

In addition to the people around you, your physical environment also plays a role in shaping your mindset. Create a space that is conducive to positivity and success. This could involve decluttering, adding inspirational quotes or images, or creating a dedicated area for relaxation and reflection.

Creating and maintaining a positive mindset is essential for success in all areas of life. By harnessing the power of NLP techniques such as reframing, anchoring, visualization, and gratitude, you can cultivate a positive mindset that empowers you to overcome challenges, achieve your goals, and live a fulfilling life. Remember, your mindset is within your control, and with NLP, you have the tools to unlock your potential and create the life you desire.

THE MINDTECH
INSTITUTE

Now, you can become a fully qualified Hypnotherapist, NLP Master Practitioner, Master Life Coach, Counsellor and more by simply studying online. More accredited Diplomas (Associate Degrees) and other courses are also available at www.themindtechinstitute.com

www.mti.edu.au

CHAPTER SEVEN
RELATIONSHIP MASTERY

Understanding Relationship Dynamics

In our journey through life, relationships play a vital role in shaping our experiences and overall well-being. Whether it's our relationships with family, friends, romantic partners, or colleagues, understanding the dynamics at play can greatly enhance our ability to connect, communicate, and build meaningful connections. Neuro-Linguistic Programming (NLP) offers powerful tools and insights that can help us navigate the complexities of relationships and foster healthy, fulfilling connections.

At its core, NLP recognizes that each individual has their own unique way of perceiving and experiencing the world. This understanding forms the foundation for understanding relationship dynamics. By acknowledging and respecting these differences, we can cultivate empathy, compassion, and effective communication.

One key aspect of relationship dynamics is the concept of rapport. Rapport refers to the deep sense of connection and understanding that is established between individuals. It is the foundation upon which trust, cooperation, and mutual respect are built. NLP provides techniques to establish and maintain rapport, allowing us to create harmonious relationships in both personal and professional settings.

Effective communication is another crucial element in relationship dynamics. NLP offers a range of tools and strategies to enhance our communication skills, enabling us to express ourselves clearly and listen attentively. By becoming aware of our own communication patterns and learning to adapt them to suit the needs of others, we can bridge the gap between different communication styles and foster deeper connections.

Understanding and managing emotions is also essential in relationship dynamics. NLP teaches us to recognize and regulate our own emotions, as well as empathize with the emotions of others. By developing emotional intelligence, we can navigate conflicts, resolve misunderstandings, and create a supportive environment for growth and connection.

Conflict is an inevitable part of any relationship, but how we handle it can make all the difference. NLP provides techniques for resolving conflicts in a constructive and respectful manner. By reframing our perspectives, actively listening to the concerns of others, and seeking win-win solutions, we can transform conflicts into opportunities for growth and understanding.

Building trust and intimacy is another vital aspect of relationship dynamics. Trust forms the foundation of any healthy relationship, and NLP offers strategies to cultivate trust and strengthen the bond between individuals. By practicing authenticity, maintaining open lines of communication, and honoring commitments, we can create a safe and nurturing environment where intimacy can flourish.

In addition to understanding the dynamics between individuals, NLP also emphasizes the importance of self-awareness and self-care in relationships. By taking responsibility for our own thoughts, emotions, and actions, we can contribute positively to our relationships and avoid projecting our own insecurities onto others. NLP techniques such as visualization and mental rehearsal can help us cultivate a positive mindset and overcome any limiting beliefs that may hinder our ability to form healthy connections.

Ultimately, understanding relationship dynamics through the lens of NLP allows us to cultivate deeper connections, resolve conflicts, and create harmonious relationships in all areas of our lives. By applying the principles and techniques of NLP, we can unlock our potential for successful and fulfilling relationships, both personally and professionally.

In the next section, we will explore effective communication in relationships and how NLP can enhance our ability to connect and understand others on a deeper level.

Effective Communication in Relationships

Effective communication is the cornerstone of any successful relationship. Whether it's with your partner, family members, friends, or colleagues, the ability to communicate effectively can make or break the connection you have with others. In this section, we will explore how Neuro-Linguistic Programming (NLP) can enhance your communication skills and help you build stronger and more fulfilling relationships.

The Power of Language

Language is a powerful tool that shapes our thoughts, beliefs, and actions. The words we choose to use can have a profound impact on how others perceive us and how we perceive ourselves. NLP teaches us to be mindful of the language we use and to choose our words carefully.

One of the key principles of NLP is the idea that the meaning of communication is the response it elicits. This means that the way we communicate can either create understanding and connection or lead to confusion and conflict. By becoming aware of the impact our words have on others, we can adjust our communication style to foster better relationships.

Building Rapport

Building rapport is an essential skill in effective communication. Rapport is the ability to establish a connection with someone, to create a sense of trust and understanding. NLP provides techniques to build rapport quickly and effortlessly.

One powerful technique is mirroring and matching. Mirroring involves subtly imitating the other person's body language, gestures, and speech patterns. Matching involves using similar words, tone of voice, and pace of speech. By mirroring and matching, you can create a sense of familiarity and similarity, which helps to establish rapport.

Another technique is pacing and leading. Pacing involves matching the other person's behavior and then gradually leading them towards a desired outcome. For example, if someone is speaking softly, you can match their volume and then gradually increase your volume to lead them towards a more assertive communication style.

Active Listening

Effective communication is not just about speaking; it also

involves active listening. Active listening is the art of fully engaging with the speaker and understanding their message. NLP provides techniques to enhance your listening skills and improve your ability to understand others.

One technique is called "meta-modeling." Meta-modeling involves asking specific questions to clarify and expand upon the speaker's message. By asking questions such as "What specifically do you mean?" or "Can you give me an example?", you can encourage the speaker to provide more detailed information, leading to a deeper understanding of their perspective.

Another technique is called "sensory acuity." Sensory acuity involves paying attention to the speaker's non-verbal cues, such as facial expressions, body language, and tone of voice. By being attuned to these cues, you can gain valuable insights into the speaker's emotions and intentions, allowing for a more empathetic and effective response.

Persuasive Language Patterns

In any relationship, there will be times when you need to persuade or influence others. NLP offers a range of persuasive language patterns that can help you communicate your ideas effectively and ethically.

One powerful pattern is called "embedded commands." Embedded commands involve subtly embedding a command within a sentence, using tonal emphasis or specific language patterns. For example, instead of saying "You should try this," you can say "You can try this and notice how it benefits you."

Another pattern is called "future pacing." Future pacing involves describing a future scenario in vivid detail, using sensory language to engage the listener's imagination. By painting a compelling picture of the desired outcome, you can inspire others to take action and make positive changes.

Resolving Conflicts

Conflict is a natural part of any relationship, but how we handle conflicts can determine the strength and longevity of the relationship. NLP provides strategies for resolving conflicts in a constructive and respectful manner.

One technique is called "reframing." Reframing involves shifting the perspective of a conflict to find a more positive and empowering interpretation. By reframing the situation, you can create a shared understanding and find common ground for resolution.

Another technique is called "chunking up." Chunking up involves zooming out from the specific details of a conflict to identify the underlying values and beliefs that are driving the disagreement. By focusing on shared values, you can find solutions that align with both parties' needs and aspirations.

Building Trust and Intimacy

Trust and intimacy are the foundation of any deep and meaningful relationship. NLP offers techniques to build trust and intimacy by fostering open and honest communication.

One technique is called "matching and mismatching." Matching involves aligning your communication style with the other person's, while mismatching involves introducing subtle differences. By matching and mismatching, you can create a sense of familiarity and novelty, which can deepen the connection and build trust.

Another technique is called "meta-programs." Meta-programs are the unconscious filters through which we perceive and respond to the world. By understanding your own and others' meta-programs, you can tailor your communication to meet their needs and preferences, creating a sense of understanding and acceptance.

In conclusion, effective communication is vital for building and maintaining strong relationships. By applying the principles and techniques of NLP, you can enhance your communication skills, build rapport, actively listen, use persuasive language patterns, resolve conflicts, and build trust and intimacy. By mastering effective communication, you can unlock the full potential of your relationships and create a more fulfilling and harmonious life.

Resolving Conflicts

Conflict is an inevitable part of life. Whether it's a disagreement with a colleague at work, a misunderstanding with a loved one, or a difference of opinion with a friend, conflicts can arise in various aspects of our lives. However, the way we handle these conflicts can greatly impact the quality of our relationships and our overall well-being. In this section, we will explore how Neuro-Linguistic Programming (NLP) can be used as a powerful tool for resolving conflicts and fostering healthy relationships.

Understanding the Nature of Conflict

Before we delve into the strategies for resolving conflicts, it's important to understand the nature of conflict itself. Conflict arises when there is a perceived incompatibility of goals, interests, or values between individuals or groups. It often involves a clash of perspectives, emotions, and communication styles. Conflict can be both internal, within ourselves, or external, between individuals or groups.

NLP provides us with valuable insights into the underlying dynamics of conflict. It helps us recognize that conflicts are not solely based on the objective reality of a situation, but are heavily influenced by our subjective perceptions, beliefs, and past experiences. By understanding this, we can begin to approach conflicts with a more open mind and a willingness to explore alternative perspectives.

The NLP Approach to Conflict Resolution

NLP offers a range of techniques and strategies that can be applied to effectively resolve conflicts. These techniques are rooted in the principles of effective communication, empathy, and understanding. Let's explore some of these strategies:

1. Active Listening: One of the fundamental skills in conflict resolution is active listening. NLP teaches us to listen not only to the words being spoken but also to the underlying emotions and intentions behind them. By actively listening, we can demonstrate empathy and create a safe space for open dialogue. This involves giving our full attention, maintaining eye contact, and using non-verbal cues to show that we are fully engaged in the conversation.

2. Reframing: Reframing is a powerful NLP technique that involves shifting our perspective on a conflict. It allows us to see the situation from a different angle, which can help us find common ground and identify mutually beneficial solutions. By reframing the conflict, we can transform it from a win-lose scenario to a win-win opportunity for both parties involved.

3. Meta-Modeling: The meta-model is a linguistic tool in NLP that helps us uncover the underlying assumptions and generalizations in our communication. By using the meta-model, we can ask specific questions to clarify vague or distorted statements, challenge limiting beliefs, and encourage more precise and effective communication. This can be particularly useful in resolving conflicts where miscommunication or misunderstandings are common.

4. Anchoring Emotional States: Conflicts often evoke strong emotions, which can hinder effective communication and problem-solving. NLP offers techniques for anchoring positive emotional states that can be accessed during conflict resolution. By anchoring positive emotions such as calmness, empathy, and understanding, we can create a more conducive environment for resolving conflicts and finding mutually agreeable solutions.

5. Rapport Building: Building rapport is essential in conflict resolution. NLP provides us with techniques to establish rapport with others, even in challenging situations. By mirroring and matching the non-verbal cues, language patterns, and physiology of the other person, we can create a sense of connection and trust. This can help to diffuse tension and create a more collaborative atmosphere for resolving conflicts.

6. Negotiation and Win-Win Solutions: NLP emphasizes the importance of seeking win-win solutions in conflicts. Instead of approaching conflicts as a zero-sum game where one party must lose for the other to win, NLP encourages us to explore creative solutions that meet the needs and interests of all parties involved. By adopting a collaborative mindset and focusing on shared goals, we can find solutions that satisfy everyone's needs and foster long-term harmony.

Applying NLP in Conflict Resolution

To effectively apply NLP techniques in conflict resolution, it's important to approach conflicts with an open mind and a genuine desire to understand and resolve the underlying issues. Here are some steps to guide you:

Recognize and acknowledge the conflict: Start by acknowledging that a conflict exists and accepting that it needs to be addressed. Avoid denying or avoiding the conflict, as this can lead to further escalation.

Practice active listening: Listen attentively to the other person's perspective, without interrupting or judging. Show empathy and seek to understand their underlying needs and concerns.

Reframe the conflict: Look for alternative perspectives and reframing opportunities. Consider how the conflict can be transformed into an opportunity for growth and understanding.

Use effective communication techniques: Apply the

principles of effective communication, such as using "I" statements, avoiding blame or criticism, and focusing on the issue at hand rather than personal attacks.

Seek win-win solutions: Collaborate with the other person to find mutually agreeable solutions that address the needs and interests of both parties. Be open to compromise and creative problem-solving.

Practice self-awareness: Be aware of your own emotions, triggers, and communication patterns during the conflict. Use anchoring techniques to access positive emotional states and maintain a calm and constructive demeanor.

Seek professional help if needed: In some cases, conflicts may be deeply rooted or complex, requiring the assistance of a trained mediator or therapist. Don't hesitate to seek professional help if the conflict persists or escalates.

By applying these NLP strategies and techniques, you can effectively resolve conflicts and foster healthier, more harmonious relationships in all areas of your life.

Remember, conflict is an opportunity for growth and understanding. By embracing the principles of NLP and approaching conflicts with empathy, open-mindedness, and effective communication, you can transform conflicts into catalysts for personal and interpersonal development.

Building Trust and Intimacy

Building trust and intimacy is essential for creating strong and meaningful relationships. Whether it's in your personal life or professional career, the ability to establish trust and foster intimacy can greatly enhance your interactions and connections with others. In this section, we will explore how Neuro-Linguistic Programming (NLP) can be used to build trust and intimacy, allowing you to create deeper and more fulfilling relationships.

Understanding Trust

Trust is the foundation of any successful relationship. It is the belief that someone is reliable, honest, and has your best interests at heart. Without trust, relationships can become strained and fragile. NLP offers powerful techniques to help you build trust and strengthen your connections with others.

Building Rapport

Rapport is the key to establishing trust and intimacy. It is the ability to create a sense of connection and understanding with another person. NLP provides various tools and techniques to help you build rapport quickly and effectively.

One such technique is mirroring and matching. This involves subtly mirroring the other person's body language, tone of voice, and even their breathing patterns. By doing so, you create a sense of familiarity and similarity, which can help establish trust and rapport.

Another technique is pacing and leading. This involves initially matching the other person's behavior and then gradually leading them towards a desired outcome. By pacing their thoughts and emotions, you create a sense of understanding and empathy, which can deepen the level of trust and intimacy in the relationship.

Effective Communication

Effective communication is crucial for building trust and intimacy. NLP offers a range of techniques to enhance your communication skills and create deeper connections with others.

One such technique is active listening. This involves fully engaging with the other person, paying attention to their words, body language, and emotions. By actively listening, you demonstrate that you value and respect the other person, which can help build trust and intimacy.

Another technique is using persuasive language patterns. NLP provides various linguistic tools to influence and persuade others in a positive and ethical way. By using these language patterns, you can create a sense of trust and understanding, leading to deeper connections and intimacy.

Emotional Intelligence

Emotional intelligence plays a vital role in building trust and intimacy. It is the ability to recognize, understand, and manage your own emotions, as well as the emotions of others. NLP offers techniques to enhance your emotional intelligence, allowing you to navigate relationships with greater ease and effectiveness.

One such technique is reframing. This involves shifting your perspective and finding alternative meanings or interpretations for a situation. By reframing, you can create a more positive and empathetic understanding of others, which can foster trust and intimacy.

Another technique is managing your own emotions. NLP provides tools to help you regulate your emotions and respond in a more constructive and empathetic manner. By managing your emotions effectively, you can create a safe and supportive environment for building trust and intimacy.

Creating Boundaries

Establishing clear boundaries is essential for building trust and intimacy. NLP offers techniques to help you set and communicate your boundaries effectively, allowing you to create healthy and respectful relationships.

One such technique is the "swish" pattern. This involves visualizing a desired boundary and mentally "swishing" it into place. By repeatedly practicing this technique, you can reinforce your boundaries and communicate them assertively, which can enhance trust and intimacy in your relationships.

Building Intimacy

Intimacy is the deep emotional connection that exists between individuals. NLP provides techniques to help you cultivate intimacy and create more meaningful relationships.

One such technique is visualization and mental rehearsal. This involves mentally rehearsing positive and intimate interactions with others. By visualizing these scenarios, you can enhance your ability to connect deeply with others, fostering trust and intimacy.

Another technique is building rapport through shared values and beliefs. By identifying and aligning your values and beliefs with others, you can create a sense of shared understanding and connection, which can deepen the level of trust and intimacy in your relationships.

Building trust and intimacy is essential for creating strong and fulfilling relationships. NLP offers a range of techniques to help you establish trust, foster intimacy, and create deeper connections with others. By applying these techniques, you can enhance your relationships both personally and professionally, leading to greater success and fulfillment in life and career.

CHAPTER EIGHT

TAKING NLP TO THE NEXT LEVEL

Regression Therapy

In the realm of hypnosis - Neuro-Linguistic Programming (NLP), there exists a powerful technique known as Regression Therapy. This technique allows individuals to access and transform their past experiences, release negative emotions, and create a compelling future. By understanding and working with the concept of time, Regression Therapy provides a unique approach to personal growth and transformation. Regression Therapy used to be part of the NLP training program, however, since it requires a hypnotic induction and understanding the levels of the mind including somnambulism it became part of the hypnosis/hypnotherapy training program at The MindTech Institute. It provides a tremendous amount of information by moving back and forth in time, and sometimes back to the womb and even to past lives to help individuals moving on in their lives to achieve their personal success. For more information about the Regression Therapy you can visit themindtechinstitute.com.

Understanding the Concept of Time

Time is a fundamental aspect of human experience. We perceive time as a linear progression, with events occurring in a sequential order from the past, through the present, and into the future. However, our perception of time is not limited to the physical world. Within our minds, we construct a mental representation of time known as our timeline.

Our timeline is a subjective representation of our past, present, and future experiences. It is the way we organize and store memories, emotions, and expectations. Understanding and working with our timeline can have a profound impact on our ability to create change and achieve success in various areas of our lives.

The Power of Regression Therapy

Regression Therapy is a technique that allows individuals to access and reframe past experiences, release negative emotions, and create a compelling future. By working with the timeline, we can gain insights into the root causes of our current challenges and transform our perception of past events.

One of the key principles of Regression Therapy is that our experiences are not fixed in time. Our memories and emotions associated with past events can be altered and reframed, leading to a shift in our present state and future outcomes. This technique enables individuals to let go of limiting beliefs, negative emotions, and unhelpful patterns of behavior that may be holding them back from achieving their goals.

The Process of Regression Therapy

The process of Regression Therapy involves accessing and working with our timeline to create positive change. Here is a step-by-step guide to the process:

Accessing the Timeline: The first step is to access the timeline within our minds. This can be done through a guided visualization or by mentally representing the timeline in front of us.

Identifying the Root Cause: Once the timeline is accessed, we can identify the root cause of a particular issue or challenge. This involves exploring past events and experiences that may have contributed to the current situation.

Reframing the Past: With the root cause identified, we can reframe the past by changing our perception of the event. This may involve altering the meaning we attach to the experience or gaining a new perspective on the situation.

Releasing Negative Emotions: the Regression Therapy provides a powerful technique for releasing negative emotions associated with past events. By revisiting the event and releasing the emotions attached to it, we can free ourselves from the emotional baggage that may be holding us back.

Creating a Compelling Future: Once the past has been reframed and negative emotions released, we can create a compelling future. This involves setting clear goals and visualizing ourselves achieving them. By aligning our timeline with our desired outcomes, we can create a powerful vision for our future.

Applications of the Regression Therapy

The Regression Therapy can be applied to various areas of life and has the potential to bring about profound transformation. Here are some examples of how the Regression Therapy can be used:

Healing Past Traumas: By reframing past traumatic experiences, individuals can release the emotional impact of the event and move forward with their lives.

Overcoming Limiting Beliefs: The Regression Therapy can help individuals identify and reframe limiting beliefs that may be holding them back from achieving their goals.

Improving Relationships: By working with the timeline, individuals can release negative emotions and patterns of behavior that may be affecting their relationships. This can lead to improved communication, trust, and intimacy.

Enhancing Performance: The Regression Therapy can be used to enhance performance in various areas, such as sports, public speaking, or career development. By aligning the timeline with desired outcomes, individuals can tap into their full potential.

Conclusion

The Regression Therapy is a powerful technique within the realm of hypnotic Neuro-Linguistic Programming that allows individuals to access and transform their past experiences, release negative emotions, and create a compelling future. By understanding and working with the concept of time, individuals can gain insights into the root causes of their challenges and create positive change in various areas of their lives. Whether it is healing past traumas, overcoming limiting beliefs, improving relationships, or enhancing performance, Regression Therapy offers a unique approach to personal growth and transformation.

Modelling Excellence

In the world of Neuro-Linguistic Programming (NLP), one of the most powerful techniques is known as "modelling excellence."

This technique involves studying and replicating the strategies and behaviors of individuals who have achieved outstanding success in a particular area of life. By understanding and adopting their mindset, beliefs, and actions, we can unlock our own potential and achieve similar levels of excellence.

Modelling excellence is based on the belief that success leaves clues. By observing and analyzing the patterns and strategies of successful individuals, we can uncover the underlying principles that contribute to their achievements. These principles can then be applied to our own lives and endeavors, allowing us to replicate their success.

The process of modelling excellence begins with identifying a role model or someone who has achieved the level of success we desire. This could be a business leader, an athlete, an artist, or anyone who has excelled in their field. Once we have identified our role model, we can start studying their mindset, beliefs, values, and behaviors.

One of the key aspects of modelling excellence is understanding the internal processes of our role model. This involves examining their thoughts, emotions, and beliefs that drive their actions. By understanding their internal world, we can gain insights into the mindset and strategies that contribute to their success.

To model excellence effectively, it is important to pay attention to both the conscious and unconscious processes of our role model. This means observing not only their overt behaviors but also their subtle cues, body language, and non-verbal communication. By studying these aspects, we can gain a deeper understanding of their strategies and incorporate them into our own lives.

Once we have gathered enough information about our role model, the next step is to start applying their strategies and behaviors in our own lives. This involves adopting their mindset, beliefs, and actions and integrating them into our daily routines. By consistently practicing these strategies, we can start to see positive changes and improvements in our own performance.

Modelling excellence is not about blindly copying someone else's actions. It is about understanding the underlying principles and adapting them to our own unique circumstances. It is about taking what works for our role model and tailoring it to suit our own goals and aspirations.

One of the key benefits of modelling excellence is that it allows us to bypass the trial-and-error process. Instead of reinventing the wheel, we can learn from those who have already achieved success and fast-track our own progress. By adopting the strategies and behaviors of successful individuals, we can avoid common pitfalls and accelerate our own growth and development.

Modelling excellence is not limited to a specific area of life. It can be applied to any aspect, whether it is health, wealth, career, relationships, or personal development. By studying and replicating the strategies of successful individuals in these areas, we can unlock our own potential and achieve extraordinary results.

In the realm of business, for example, we can model the leadership and communication styles of successful entrepreneurs. By understanding how they inspire and motivate their teams, we can become more effective leaders ourselves. Similarly, in the field of health and wellness, we can model the habits and behaviors of individuals who have achieved optimal well-being. By adopting their healthy lifestyle choices, we can improve our own physical and mental well-being.

Modelling excellence is not a one-time process. It is an ongoing journey of growth and development. As we continue to learn and evolve, we can seek out new role models and expand our repertoire of strategies and behaviors. By constantly refining and adapting our approach, we can continue to unlock our potential and achieve greater levels of success in all areas of life.

In conclusion, modelling excellence is a powerful technique within the realm of Neuro-Linguistic Programming (NLP) that allows us to study and replicate the strategies and behaviors of successful individuals. By understanding and adopting their mindset, beliefs, and actions, we can unlock our own potential and achieve similar levels of excellence. Whether it is in business, health, relationships, or personal development, modelling excellence can be applied to any area of life. By consistently practicing the strategies of successful individuals, we can fast-track our own growth and achieve extraordinary results.

Strategies for Success

In the previous sections, we have explored the foundational principles and techniques of Neuro-Linguistic Programming (NLP) that can help you unlock your potential and achieve success in various areas of your life. Now, let's delve deeper into some powerful strategies that can further enhance your success using NLP.

1. Setting Well-Formed Outcomes: One of the key strategies for success in any endeavor is setting well-formed outcomes. NLP provides a structured approach to goal setting that increases the likelihood of achieving your desired outcomes. By using the SMART criteria (Specific, Measurable, Achievable, Relevant, and Time-bound), you can create clear and compelling goals that align with your values and motivate you to take action.

2. Utilizing Strategies for Excellence: NLP emphasizes the importance of modeling excellence. By studying and replicating the strategies of successful individuals in your field, you can accelerate your own progress. Identify someone who has achieved the level of success you desire and study their mindset, behaviors, and communication patterns. By adopting their strategies, you can enhance your own performance and achieve similar results.

3. Reframing Limiting Beliefs: Our beliefs shape our reality and influence our actions. NLP offers powerful techniques for reframing limiting beliefs that hold you back from reaching your full potential. By challenging and replacing negative beliefs with empowering ones, you can overcome self-doubt and develop a mindset that supports your success. Reframing allows you to see obstacles as opportunities and setbacks as learning experiences.

4. Anchoring Success States: Anchoring is a technique in NLP that allows you to access resourceful states at will. By associating a specific gesture, word, or image with a positive emotional state, you can create an anchor that triggers that state whenever you need it. For example, if you want to feel confident before a presentation, you can anchor that state by pressing your thumb and index finger together. By anchoring success states, you can quickly shift your mindset and perform at your best in any situation.

5. Using Language Patterns for Influence: Language is a powerful tool for communication and influence. NLP provides a range of language patterns that can help you effectively convey your message and influence others. By using techniques such as embedded commands, presuppositions, and metaphors, you can subtly guide the thoughts and behaviors of others towards your desired outcomes. Mastering persuasive language patterns can greatly enhance your ability to negotiate, lead, and inspire others.

6. Developing Rapport: Rapport is the foundation of effective communication and building strong relationships. NLP offers techniques for establishing rapport quickly and effortlessly. By matching and mirroring the physiology, voice tone, and language of the person you are communicating with, you can create a sense of connection and trust. Developing rapport allows you to better understand others, resolve conflicts, and collaborate effectively.

7. Utilizing Visualization and Mental Rehearsal: Visualization and mental rehearsal are powerful techniques used by athletes, performers, and successful individuals in various fields. NLP provides structured processes for harnessing the power of your imagination to create compelling visions of success. By vividly imagining yourself achieving your goals and rehearsing the necessary actions, you can enhance your confidence, motivation, and performance. Visualization and mental rehearsal help you align your subconscious mind with your conscious goals, increasing the likelihood of success.

8. Practicing Self-Reflection and Feedback: Self-reflection and feedback are essential for personal growth and continuous improvement. NLP encourages regular self-reflection to identify patterns, beliefs, and behaviors that may be hindering your success. By seeking feedback from trusted mentors, coaches, or peers, you can gain valuable insights and perspectives that can help you refine your strategies and overcome challenges. Embracing a growth mindset and being open to feedback allows you to adapt and evolve on your journey to success.

9. Taking Action and Embracing Failure: Success is not solely determined by knowledge or intention; it requires consistent action. NLP emphasizes the importance of taking action and learning from both successes and failures. Embrace failure as an opportunity for growth and learning. By adopting a mindset of experimentation and resilience, you can overcome obstacles and move closer to your goals. Remember, every failure brings you one step closer to success.

10. Seeking Support and Continuous Learning: Finally, to maximize your success with NLP, seek support from like-minded individuals and continue to expand your knowledge and skills. Join NLP communities, attend workshops, and engage in ongoing learning. Surround yourself with individuals who inspire and challenge you to grow. By immersing yourself in a supportive environment and continuously expanding your understanding of NLP, you can unlock your full potential and achieve extraordinary success.

Incorporating these strategies into your life and career can significantly enhance your success using Neuro-Linguistic Programming. Remember, NLP is a powerful tool, but it is your commitment, dedication, and consistent application of these strategies that will ultimately determine your level of success. Embrace the power of NLP, and unlock your potential for a fulfilling and successful life and career.

NLP in Coaching and Therapy

Neuro-Linguistic Programming (NLP) has proven to be an incredibly powerful tool in the fields of coaching and therapy. By understanding and utilizing the principles and techniques of NLP, coaches and therapists can help their clients achieve profound personal transformation and overcome various challenges.

The Role of NLP in Coaching

Coaching is a collaborative process that aims to help individuals achieve their goals and unlock their full potential. NLP provides coaches with a comprehensive set of tools and techniques to facilitate this process effectively.

One of the key aspects of NLP in coaching is the ability to establish rapport with clients. Rapport is the foundation of any successful coaching relationship, as it creates trust and openness between the coach and the client. NLP offers various techniques, such as mirroring and matching, to establish and maintain rapport effortlessly.

NLP also provides coaches with powerful questioning techniques to help clients gain clarity and insight into their goals, values, and beliefs. By asking the right questions, coaches can help clients uncover limiting beliefs and reframe them into empowering ones. This process allows clients to overcome obstacles and move forward towards their desired outcomes.

Another valuable aspect of NLP in coaching is the ability to help clients set compelling goals. NLP techniques, such as the well-formed outcome and the SMART goal-setting model, enable coaches to guide clients in creating clear, specific, and achievable goals. By aligning their goals with their values and beliefs, clients are more likely to stay motivated and committed to their desired outcomes.

NLP also offers powerful techniques for managing emotions and creating empowering habits. Coaches can help clients identify and reframe negative emotions, such as fear or self-doubt, into more resourceful states. Additionally, coaches can assist clients in creating new habits that support their goals and lead to long-term success.

NLP in Therapy

NLP techniques have also been widely used in the field of therapy to help individuals overcome various psychological challenges and achieve personal growth.

One of the primary applications of NLP in therapy is the process of reframing. Reframing involves helping clients reinterpret their experiences and view them from a different perspective. By reframing negative experiences, clients can change their emotional responses and develop more empowering beliefs and behaviors.

NLP also offers effective techniques for managing and transforming limiting beliefs. Through techniques such as the belief change pattern and the swish pattern, therapists can help clients identify and replace limiting beliefs with more empowering ones. This process allows clients to break free from self-imposed limitations and create new possibilities for themselves.

Another valuable aspect of NLP in therapy is the use of visualization and mental rehearsal. These techniques involve guiding clients to vividly imagine themselves achieving their desired outcomes and rehearsing the necessary steps to get there. By engaging the power of the subconscious mind, clients can enhance their motivation, confidence, and belief in their ability to achieve their goals.

NLP techniques can also be used to help clients overcome phobias and traumas. Techniques such as the fast phobia cure and the timeline therapy can assist clients in releasing negative emotions associated with past traumatic experiences. By reprogramming their responses to these triggers, clients can experience profound healing and emotional freedom.

Integrating NLP into Coaching and Therapy

Integrating NLP into coaching and therapy requires a deep understanding of the principles and techniques of NLP, as well as the ability to adapt them to the specific needs of each client.

Coaches and therapists who incorporate NLP into their practice often undergo specialized training to enhance their skills and knowledge in this field. This training equips them with a wide range of tools and techniques that can be tailored to meet the unique needs of their clients.

By integrating NLP into their coaching and therapy sessions, practitioners can help their clients achieve rapid and lasting change. NLP provides a holistic approach that addresses the underlying patterns of behavior and thinking, allowing clients to make profound shifts in their lives.

Whether it's helping clients overcome limiting beliefs, managing emotions, setting compelling goals, or enhancing communication skills, NLP offers a powerful framework for coaches and therapists to facilitate personal transformation and empower their clients to achieve success in all areas of their lives.

In conclusion, NLP has proven to be an invaluable tool in the fields of coaching and therapy. By incorporating NLP techniques into their practice, coaches and therapists can help their clients achieve profound personal transformation, overcome challenges, and unlock their full potential. The principles and techniques of NLP provide a comprehensive framework for facilitating change and empowering individuals to create success, health, wealth, and fulfilling relationships in their lives.

CONCLUSION

As we come to the end of this transformative journey through the power of the subconscious mind, it is important to take a moment to reflect on the growth and discoveries you have experienced along the way. This final chapter serves as a reminder of the profound impact that tapping into your subconscious can have on your life and the endless possibilities for growth and success that lie before you.

Throughout this book, we have explored techniques and practices to harness the power of your subconscious mind, overcome limitations, and create a life of success and fulfillment. From understanding the role of the subconscious in shaping our reality to manifesting our desires and nurturing our well-being, each chapter has offered valuable insights and tools for personal transformation.

In this concluding chapter, we will recap and celebrate your subconscious journey, reinforcing the knowledge and understanding you have gained. We will also explore the importance of maintaining a continued relationship with your subconscious and the ongoing opportunities for growth and success that await you. Let us now embark on this final chapter, embracing the life-changing potential that lies within your subconscious mind.

Recap and Celebration of Your Subconscious Journey

Congratulations on completing your subconscious journey! Throughout this book, we have delved into the depths of the subconscious mind, exploring its power and potential. Now, let's take a moment to recap what we have learned and celebrate the transformation you have experienced.

In the early chapters, we laid the foundation by understanding the subconscious mind and its role in shaping our reality. We learned that the subconscious mind holds immense power and is responsible for much of our thoughts, actions, and outcomes. By harnessing this power, we can overcome limitations and create a life of success and fulfillment.

One key aspect of unlocking subconscious potential is identifying and reprogramming limiting beliefs and programming. We explored techniques to identify these beliefs and replace them with empowering ones. Through visualization, affirmations, and techniques for accessing the subconscious, we discovered how to rewire our minds for success.

Our thoughts and emotions are deeply influenced by the subconscious. Understanding our thought patterns and addressing negative thinking and emotional blocks allows us to align our thoughts and emotions for positive change. We also explored the importance of emotional healing and growth, recognizing that the subconscious plays a significant role in our emotional well-being.

Manifesting our desires through the subconscious requires setting clear goals, creating vision boards and mind movies, and programming our subconscious mind for manifestation. We learned the importance of taking aligned action and tapping into the universal laws of attraction to manifest our goals and dreams.

Nurturing our subconscious mind is essential for overall well-being. We explored practices such as self-care, self-love, mindfulness, meditation, and cultivating positive habits and routines. Through these practices, we can enhance creativity, develop intuition, and access our subconscious potential.

Transforming relationships through the subconscious involves understanding relationship patterns, healing past wounds and trauma, and attracting healthy relationships. Effective communication and conflict resolution skills play a crucial role in building lasting connections through the subconscious.

In the realm of career and finances, aligning with our true path, overcoming money blocks and scarcity mindset, and manifesting abundance and financial success are all influenced by the subconscious. We also discovered how the subconscious can guide us in career growth and creating wealth and legacy.

The mind-body connection became evident when we explored

the role of the subconscious in mental and physical well-being. Healing the body, relieving stress, boosting energy and vitality are all areas where the power of the subconscious can be harnessed for better health.

Cultivating spirituality and higher consciousness involves exploring our spirituality, connecting with higher realms and universal wisdom, and expanding our consciousness through spiritual practices. Living a purposeful and meaningful life and evolving into higher states of consciousness are all within reach by tapping into the power of our subconscious mind.

Throughout our subconscious journey, we embraced transformation and growth. We learned to let go of resistance, overcome fear, and step into courage. Embodying personal growth and sustaining success became part of our subconscious journey. By embracing a life of fulfillment and purpose, we have truly unlocked our subconscious potential.

Now, as we conclude this book, remember that your relationship with your subconscious doesn't end here. It is a lifelong journey, and the possibilities for growth and success are endless. Continue to nurture your subconscious mind, practice the techniques and principles learned, and embrace the power within you.

Celebrate the progress you've made and reflect on how far you've come. Your subconscious journey has equipped you with the tools and knowledge to create the life you desire. Congratulations, and may your continued exploration of your subconscious mind bring you abundant joy, fulfillment, and success.

Your Continued Relationship with Your Subconscious

As you embark on a journey to unlock the power of your subconscious mind, it is important to understand that this is not a one-time event or a quick fix. Your relationship with your subconscious is an ongoing process of exploration, growth, and development. Just like any other relationship, it requires nurturing, attention, and regular maintenance.

To continue building a strong and harmonious relationship with your subconscious, it is crucial to integrate the techniques and practices you have learned into your daily life. Consistency is key. Here are some ways to foster a deep and lasting connection with your subconscious mind:

1. *Daily Affirmations:* Affirmations are positive statements that resonate with your subconscious mind and help reprogram limiting beliefs and negative thought patterns. By repeating affirmations daily, you reinforce new empowering beliefs and build a stronger connection with your subconscious. For example, you may affirm, "I am worthy of love, success, and abundance" to counteract any feelings of unworthiness or scarcity mindset.

2.   *Visualization and Mental Rehearsal:* Visualization is a powerful technique that utilizes the imagination to create vivid mental images of your desired outcomes. By visualizing your goals and aspirations as already achieved, you activate your subconscious mind and align it with your conscious intentions. For instance, if your goal is to become a successful entrepreneur, you can visualize yourself confidently running your own thriving business, experiencing the joy and fulfillment it brings.

3.   *Journaling and Mindfulness:* Keeping a journal allows you to tap into the depths of your subconscious mind by capturing your thoughts, emotions, and experiences on paper. This practice enhances self-awareness and helps you identify patterns, triggers, and areas for growth. Practicing mindfulness, such as meditation or deep breathing exercises, can also help you cultivate a deep connection with your subconscious by quieting the conscious mind and allowing the subconscious to take center stage.

4.   *Listening to Your Intuition:* Your intuition is the voice of your subconscious, guiding you towards what feels aligned and authentic. To strengthen your intuitive abilities, it is important to create space for stillness and listen to the whispers of your inner wisdom. Trusting your gut feelings and acting upon them allows you to deepen your connection with your subconscious and make decisions that are in alignment with your true self.

5.   *Continuing Education and Growth:* The more you learn about the power of the subconscious mind, the better equipped you will be to harness its potential. Read books, attend workshops, and listen to podcasts that expand your knowledge and understanding. By continually seeking new insights and techniques, you will be able to deepen your relationship with your subconscious and discover new ways to leverage its power.

Remember that your relationship with your subconscious is unique to you. Explore different practices, techniques, and modalities to find what resonates with you the most. As you continue to nurture this relationship, be patient and gentle with yourself. Transformation takes time, and each step along the way is an opportunity for growth and self-discovery.

By cultivating an ongoing and intimate relationship with your subconscious mind, you will unlock its infinite potential and create a life of fulfillment, success, and meaning.

The Endless Possibilities for Growth and Success

As you have journeyed through the exploration of your subconscious mind, you have likely begun to realize the incredible potential it holds for your personal growth and success. The possibilities for transformation and achievement are truly endless when you tap into the power of your subconscious.

One of the most exciting aspects of unlocking your subconscious mind is discovering the ability to reprogram limiting beliefs and patterns of behavior. Through techniques such as affirmations, visualization, and reprogramming, you can replace negative thoughts and self-sabotaging behaviors with positive, empowering ones. This opens up a world of new opportunities and allows you to reach greater heights in all areas of your life.

For example, imagine you have always believed that you are not good enough and that success is reserved for others. This limiting belief has held you back from pursuing your dreams and taking risks. However, once you become aware of this belief and work to reprogram it, you can start affirming positive statements such as "I am capable of achieving great things" or "I am deserving of success." By consistently reinforcing these new beliefs, you begin to attract opportunities that align with your desires and propel you towards success.

Additionally, the power of the subconscious mind can greatly impact your ability to manifest your desires. By setting clear goals, creating vision boards, and using techniques like mind movies, you can program your subconscious to align with your aspirations. The subconscious mind then works behind the scenes, influencing your thoughts, actions, and decisions to bring your desires into reality.

For instance, suppose you have always dreamed of starting your own business but have never taken the leap due to fear of failure. By visualizing yourself as a successful entrepreneur, using affirmations to boost your confidence, and programming your subconscious for abundance and success, you gradually build the inner belief and motivation necessary to take action. As a result, you begin to attract the right resources, opportunities, and support to turn your business idea into a flourishing reality.

The power of the subconscious mind also extends to your relationships, career, finances, and overall well-being. By harnessing this power, you can improve communication and resolve conflicts in your relationships, align with your true career path, overcome financial limitations, enhance your mental and physical health, and cultivate a deeper connection with your spirituality.

There are countless stories of individuals who have tapped into the power of their subconscious mind and achieved extraordinary success. The MindTech Institute, a renowned institute that qualifies Master Life Coaches, emphasizes the importance of mastering the mind and the power of belief in achieving one's goals. They have helped countless individuals overcome limitations and create lives of fulfillment and abundance.

Moreover, several scientific studies have demonstrated the effectiveness of techniques like visualization and affirmations in achieving desired outcomes. For example, a study published in the Journal of Experimental Social Psychology found that visualization techniques increased participants' motivation and performance levels. Another study published in the Journal of Personality and Social Psychology showed that affirmations helped individuals overcome self-doubt and improve their problem-solving abilities.

As you continue to explore and nurture your relationship with your subconscious mind, you will discover new insights, techniques, and possibilities for growth and success. The key is to remain open-minded, consistent, and committed to your personal development journey. With the power of your subconscious mind as your ally, there is no limit to what you can achieve and the impact you can make in your own life and the lives of others.

THE MINDTECH
INSTITUTE

Now, you can become a fully qualified Hypnotherapist, NLP
Master Practitioner, Master Life Coach, Counsellor and more by
simply studying online. More accredited Diplomas (Associate
Degrees) and other courses are also available at
www.themindtechinstitute.com

www.mti.edu.au

FEW LAST WORDS

As we reach the final pages of "The Power of NLP: Rewire Your Reality," I want to express my heartfelt gratitude for joining me on this transformative journey. Throughout this book, we've explored the fascinating world of Neuro-Linguistic Programming (NLP) and its profound potential to reshape your reality.

NLP is not just a theoretical concept; it's a practical tool that empowers you to take control of your life. It's about understanding the language of your mind, rewriting the scripts that have held you back, and crafting a brighter, more fulfilling future.

But remember, this journey doesn't end here. NLP is not a destination; it's a lifelong adventure of self-discovery and growth. As you step forward, armed with the knowledge and techniques you've acquired, keep these few last words in mind:

Practice Makes Progress: Mastery of NLP, like any skill, comes with practice. Consistently apply the principles and exercises you've learned to see real change in your life.

Be Patient and Kind to Yourself: Rewiring your reality may take time. Be patient with your progress, and remember that every small step counts.

Stay Curious: The more you explore the depths of NLP, the more you'll uncover. Keep your curiosity alive and continue to expand your understanding.

Share Your Knowledge: As you experience the benefits of NLP, consider sharing your insights and techniques with others. Your journey can inspire and uplift those around you.

Learn More And go Beyond: TheMindTech Institute offers one of the top NLP Training you can find anywhere. With cutting-edge technology now you can study the whole NLP Practitioner and Master Practitioner levels and get certified totally online at your own pace. Learn more, visit: themindtechinstitute.com

With these words in mind, I encourage you to take what you've learned and embark on a life filled with purpose, abundance, and the knowledge that you have the power to shape your own reality. Thank you for being a part of this incredible journey. Your potential is limitless, and your future is yours to create. Go forth and rewire your reality with the power of NLP.

FEW WORDS OF APPRECIATION

To the incredible readers. I want to express my deepest appreciation and heartfelt gratitude. Your decision to embark on this transformative journey fills me with inspiration and joy. Your commitment to self-discovery and personal growth is truly commendable.

As you continue to explore the depths of your mind and unlock its hidden treasures, remember that every step you take is a stride toward a more empowered and fulfilling life. Challenges may arise, but within them, you'll discover opportunities for growth and transformation.

Believe in the incredible power you possess, and let it guide you towards the life you desire. Embrace each day with renewed determination and the knowledge that you have the ability to shape your reality.

Thank you for being part of this journey, and may your path be filled with success, resilience, and the unwavering belief in your own potential. Your commitment to personal growth is an inspiration to us all. Keep shining, keep exploring, and keep supercharging your mind. The best is yet to come.

With heartfelt gratitude,
Adam Musselli

ABOUT THE AUTHOR

Adam Musselli

Adam has been involved in the fields of psychology, social and behavioral science, as well as training and education since 2008. His extensive educational background, diverse experience, multilingual proficiency, and deep comprehension of human behavior, sociology, and psychology collectively form a robust foundation that informs his approach to a numerous subjects. He perceives knowledge as an indispensable part of life, and he believes in the simplicity of training and teaching.

Adam is the founder and director of The MindTech Institute. He runs several seminars, workshops and courses globally throughout the year as well as through The MindTech Institute's website: themindtechinstitute.com

Adam also covers various topics on his podcast "The Dynamic Thinking Project" which is available on iTunes, Spotify as well as all the major podcast platforms and other media broadcast outlets.

Courses That Will Change The Course Of Your Life

Discover a path to personal and career development that can help you rebuild your life. These courses offer invaluable tools and guidance to rebuild your sense of self, boost confidence, and create success strategies. They even open doors to potential income streams. By enrolling online, you gain access to these empowering courses that navigate personal success, foster resilience, and pave the way for a healthier, more fulfilling future. Study at your own pace using our user-friendly online learning system, and become fully qualified in your chosen field. It's a flexible and empowering way to regain control and shape the life you desire.

Master Life Coach Training

NLP Practitioner & NLP Master Practitioner Levels (2 in 1)

Life Coaching Training

Hypnosis Practitioner & Master Practitioner Levels – Hypnotherapy (2 in 1)

Life Management Training

The 8 Rules Of Human Nature And Development (People's Archetypes - Values)

Advanced Sales Training

Leadership Training Program

Advanced Presentation Training

Neuro-Linguistic Programming Training (NLP) Practitioner

Neuro-Linguistic Programming Training (NLP) Master Practitioner

Hypnosis (Hypnotherapy) Training Practitioner

And many more…

www.themindtechinstitute.com **OR** www.mti.edu.au

Mind Supercharge: Unleashing Your Subconscious Power

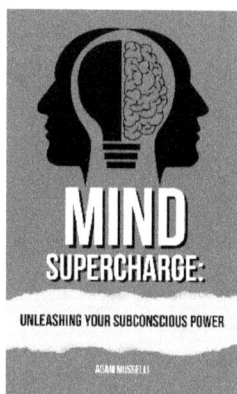

A compelling exploration into the limitless capabilities of the human mind. Authored with a deep understanding of the intricate workings of the subconscious, this book serves as a profound guide to tapping into your hidden potential and transforming your life. At the core of this enlightening journey is the revelation of the profound impact your subconscious exerts on your daily existence. From the thoughts that shape your perspective to the actions that determine your outcomes, the subconscious plays an integral role in molding your reality. This book unveils the key to unlocking and harnessing this potent force. With practical techniques and expert insights, "Mind Supercharge: Unleashing Your Subconscious Power" empowers readers to transcend their limitations.

Whether you seek personal growth, career advancement, or a deeper understanding of the human psyche, "Mind Supercharge: Unleashing Your Subconscious Power" equips you with the tools to achieve your goals. If you're ready to take charge of your life, overcome limitations, and craft a future filled with success and fulfillment, this book is your indispensable companion. It's a testament to the power of the human mind and a roadmap to a brighter, more empowered existence.

Available Now: https://themindtechinstitute.com/shop/

Tranceformation: The Hypnotist's Secret

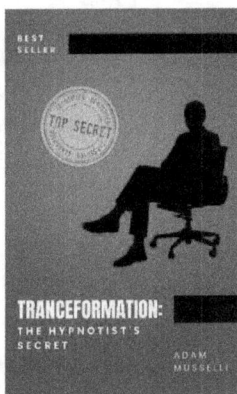

"Tranceformation: The Hypnotist's Secret" - Your Gateway to Unleashing the Power of Hypnosis and Hypnotherapy!

Are you ready to unlock the hidden potential of your mind and embark on a journey of self-discovery and transformation? Dive into the mesmerizing world of hypnosis and hypnotherapy with this groundbreaking book, "Tranceformation: The Hypnotist's Secret. "In "Tranceformation," you will embark on an extraordinary voyage into the depths of the human psyche, guided by the expertise of seasoned a psychologist ad hypnotherapist and author Adam Musselli. With over 15 years of experience in the field, Adam Musselli unveils the closely-guarded secrets of hypnosis, demystifying its profound impact on our thoughts, behaviors, and emotions."Tranceformation: The Hypnotist's Secret" is not just a book; it's your key to a life-changing journey of self-discovery. Whether you're a curious beginner or an experienced practitioner, this comprehensive guide offers valuable insights and practical exercises that will transform your life. Join the ranks of those who have experienced profound change through hypnosis and hypnotherapy. Don't miss out on this opportunity to embrace the limitless potential of your mind. Order "Tranceformation: The Hypnotist's Secret" today, and embark on your own extraordinary journey toward transformation and empowerment. Your future self will thank you.

Available Now: https://themindtechinstitute.com/shop/

When It's All Over: A Guide To Healing The Scars of Lost Love

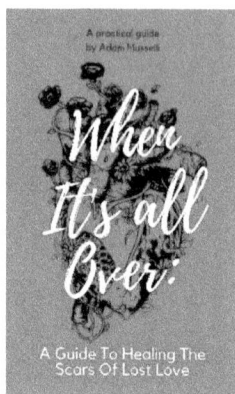

Are you tired of the pain and heartache caused by a devastating breakup? Do you find yourself longing for healing and freedom from the shackles of a broken relationship? Look no further! "When It's All Over: A Guide To Healing the Scars of Lost Love" is here to guide you on a transformative journey towards complete emotional recovery.

In this powerful eBook, you will embark on a life-changing voyage of self-discovery, growth, and healing. Through insightful guidance and proven techniques, you will learn how to turn your pain into strength and reclaim your power. Let go of the past and embrace a brighter future where your heart is unburdened and free to love again.

Through 13 thought-provoking chapters, "When It's All Over: A Guide To Healing the Scars of Lost Love" addresses the various aspects of healing from heartbreak. Each chapter is designed to empower you with practical tools and wisdom, guiding you step-by-step towards emotional liberation.

Available Now: https://themindtechinstitute.com/shop/

The Day We Gave Up Health

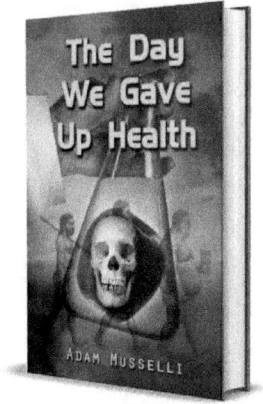

How in the world did we get so fat so fast! Obesity is now well beyond acceptable limits and it continues to rise worldwide. Even children and animals are now prone to obesity. Have we become lazier in the last few decades or is it due to our growing addiction to foods. Has global obesity become a pandemic by design or by chance? Are we, as humans, in a new phase of evolution due to the consumption of a new genre of foods and substances that are entirely foreign to our bodies? Are we going to make it as a species through this new phase or wither and die? Will we, as a species evolve and adapt to the new foods which are flooding our homes and markets? This book is the result of extensive research and analysis. The book attempts to answer some of these big questions honestly. Contributions from experts in the field of medicine, health, politics and research have been incorporated into this book to provide you with honest

facts. There is no better time than now to know the truth and what is really happening behind the scenes. The truth is here and you deserve to know it.

Available Now: https://themindtechinstitute.com/shop/

THE MINDTECH
INSTITUTE

Email: info@themindtechinstitute.com

Websites: www.themindtechinstitute.com

www.mti.edu.au

www.ingramcontent.com/pod-product-compliance
Lightning Source LLC
LaVergne TN
LVHW051600080426
835510LV00020B/3074